ALWAYS AT EASE

Also by
Christopher J. McCullough, Ph.D.
Outgrowing Agoraphobia

With Robert Woods Mann
Managing Your Anxiety

ALWAYS AT EASE

OVERCOMING SHYNESS AND ANXIETY IN EVERY SITUATION

CHRISTOPHER J. MCCULLOUGH, PH.D.

JEREMY P. TARCHER, INC.
Los Angeles

Jeremy P. Tarcher, Inc.
5858 Wilshire Blvd., Suite 200
Los Angeles, CA 90036

Distributed by St. Martin's Press, New York

Library of Congress Cataloging-in-Publication Data

McCullough, Christopher J.
Always at ease: overcoming shyness and anxiety in everyday situations/by Christopher J. McCullough.
p. cm.
ISBN 0-87477-542-6
1. Bashfulness. 2. Anxiety. I. Title.
BF575.B3M33 1991 91-9361
158'.2—dc20 CIP

Manufactured in the United States of America

To
Stephanie Bernstein
whose bright light
we miss

CONTENTS

ACKNOWLEDGMENTS

There are many to thank for their contributions to *Always at Ease*. My appreciation goes to my lovely and talented writer and friend, Suzanne Lipsett, for her work on the early ideas of this book. Gratitude goes to Rick Benzel for his tenacious editing and gentle guidance. Thanks to Philip Goldberg and Andrea Stein for their excellent editing. Many thanks to Jeremy Tarcher, my publisher, who had numerous opportunities to renew his faith in the project. To Stephanie Bernstein who brought so much life to the book and who was taken from us shortly before the book's completion. Finally, very special thanks to Sara Lou O'Connor who came in and organized everything into a real book. She did this while she also made important creative contributions to *Always at Ease*.

Preface

M any years ago I received an invitation to appear on a local television talk show to discuss my work with patients who suffer from social anxiety.

Without a second thought, I accepted. But within moments of hanging up the phone I felt a surge of apprehension. I became aware of thoughts of self-doubt—did I know enough to do a television show? Then there was a second level of concern: what if the live audience and the viewers at home actually saw this nervousness and self-doubt? "After all," I mused, "how ridiculous it would be for someone who specializes in the treatment of anxiety to be a basket case himself." That irony doubled my initial fear.

I was confronted with a potent dilemma. Canceling the appearance would bring instant relief but I'd lose an important opportunity to express my ideas and promote my new practice.

My first realization was that I could always back out—that gave me a last-resort exit of sorts. At least I wasn't trapped. But if I did decide to appear on the show, what could I do to make it easier for myself?

Finally, I forced myself to sit down and think realistically about my fears. "What's the worst that can happen?" I asked. "I guess it would be that I would make a fool of myself. I might appear so laughable that my career in the San Francisco area would be finished. What would I do then?" As I thought about that seriously, I realized that my life still would not be over. If I embarrassed myself on local television—if, for example, while describing my treatment of social anxiety, I had a panic attack myself—I could simply close my practice and move to New York. It might take years for the story to reach the East Coast! This possibility gave me a little much-needed comic relief.

Deep inside I knew I was a competent therapist whose knowledge and skills had helped many patients overcome debilitating anxieties. If on television I didn't prove to be the next Dr. Joyce Brothers, that didn't mean I was less of a person. My worth as an individual or even as a professional would not be affected. A single media appearance would not determine my future. In this way I learned to limit suffering to the situation rather than projecting it on to my whole life.

Having realistically considered the worst-case scenario, I became considerably more calm. In fact, I became more at ease with my anxiety *about* the anxiety. When it came time to make my television debut, I had some anxiety but I came off just fine. It was the first of many appearances. In fact, these days I host my own radio talk show and I recently appeared on national television with Joyce Brothers herself.

That trauma helped me understand the depth of suffering my patients feel in certain social situations. I learned firsthand what it was like to confront the choice between fear and growth.

I was also reminded of the price one pays for avoiding social anxiety; a price that, at the moment when one decides whether to run or to confront anxiety, is not fully appreciated. When I look back on my own career, I am awed by the contrast between my life as a confronter of anxiety and what it would have been like if I had avoided anxiety-provoking encounters.

One of the reasons I wrote this book was to make people aware of both the price of social avoidance and the potential for life enhancement which comes with the courage to assert yourself. Because it is so appealing to avoid discomfort and because the relief is so immediate, we overlook the huge costs of avoidance.

This book begins with the fundamental assertion that "shyness" is not the problem; rather shyness is a defense against social anxiety. Shyness, like a phobia, is not a feeling but a behavior, an attempt to avoid anxiety. By successfully shying away from people you reduce anxiety. Of course, the "treatment" of shyness comes with its own cost, but, if the price of shyness was not already too high you would probably not be reading this book.

The feeling of anxiety that underlies shyness is the real issue. However, anxiety often serves us well—from alerting us to real danger to giving our performance an enhancing boost.

The opposite state, being *at ease,* refers to an inner sense of confidence and self-esteem that we take with us into social encounters. This does not mean we are immune from anxiety, but rather that we confront the anxiety with an inner ease born of genuine self-acceptance. Simply put, people who experience disabling levels of social anxiety do not simply lack social skills but, rather, lack an adequate level of inner certitude.

Anxiety indicates that you care. Can you imagine being anxious about something that means nothing to you? It is natural to be anxious in situations which have value to you so it is hardly my purpose to ease you into a state of disinterest. The goal is to be at ease with meaningful anxiety—not to sleep through social events.

It is not hard to differentiate shyness from social anxiety. Those who are intensely shy present a fairly typical profile of behavior and characteristics. But social anxiety is more difficult to characterize. Not everyone who suffers from social anxiety suffers in the same way; what bothers one individual—initiating a conversation with a stranger for example—might not bother another. In other words, social anxiety is situationally dependent.

Of course, I did find some characteristics shared by most socially anxious people. One is difficulty in expressing feelings to others. Another is what I call *generic anxiety*—a kind of basic anxiety one has about appearance or intelligence. These ever-present generic anxieties are exacerbated in situations that arouse anxiety. Public speaking, for example, is frightening because it arouses both generic anxiety about ourselves and situational anxiety about our performance. No wonder most Americans report that they fear public speaking almost as much as dying!

To help patients who suffer from social anxiety, I developed a two-fold approach. First, I assist them in understanding how their thoughts and attitudes both create and sustain their anxious feelings. Then we address the physical symptoms which accompany these feelings. This is particularly important since the fear of one's symptoms being obvious to others exacerbates anxiety.

However, using techniques which reframe negative thinking and reshape behaviours is not enough. The goal is not to be relaxed all the time but rather to be *at ease;* to develop and maintain an inner self-acceptance in the face of social challenge. The vehicle for achieving greater self-esteem is self-assertion. Assertiveness is the antidote to disabling anxiety. And assertiveness comes from knowing how you feel and manifesting it in the world.

It *is* possible for you to always feel at ease in social situations in the sense that you can always feel at ease with yourself. True, you may not feel relaxed or comfortable all the time—but then, not all anxiety is bad. A bit of manageable anxiety before a speech can give you an extra edge of alertness. A small dose of nervousness before a date can give you an added bit of sparkle. The difference between being socially anxious and always at ease is a matter of control—are you controlling and using your anxiety, or is it controlling you?

As your social anxiety begins to ebb, you will find yourself becoming more honest with yourself and more genuine with others. By being your authentic self, you will lay the psychological foundation for social ease. And by living the truth of who you are you will discover that you can count on yourself to be always at ease.

One of the definitions of *ease* is simply "naturalness." The experience of social ease, therefore, is not something that you need to do as much as it is something you need to allow. The socially anxious person and the shy person—who avoids socially anxious encounters—are invited, through the pages of this book, to accept their genuine selves.

Chapters 1 through 7 help you to understand the nature of your social anxiety and shyness to experience social ease. Chapters 8 through 11 discuss how you can apply these insights and skills to particular social situations: in your job, in your relationships, and in social gatherings.

1 WHEN LIFE ISN'T EASY

He who knows others is learned; he who knows himself is wise.

LAO TZU

Do you often have difficulty expressing your feelings to others? Does it seem that there's part of yourself you dare not show the world? Does it seem that a part of your life will never be fully lived?

Are there particular situations in which you feel overwhelmed by anxiety? Perhaps you're afraid of being criticized? Or does giving criticism frighten you?

When you find yourself uncomfortable in certain social settings, do you remain silent for fear of making a fool of yourself? In those circumstances, do you begin to sweat, or blush, or get a tight feeling in your chest?

Do you feel tense, even dizzy when you're around certain people? Do you get a headache, or feel nauseated, or do you just feel numb in certain social or work situations?

Does it seem to you that other people somehow look better than you? Does just preparing to go out for a special occasion make you feel uncomfortable?

Do you feel ill at ease when you have to eat alone in a restaurant, complain in a store, accept a compliment, call a friend to break a date, make a speech or presentation, meet strangers, say no when asked for a favor you do not want to do or when you ask for something that someone may not wish to give you?

If any of these questions reveal your secret fears and feelings, then you're familiar with social anxiety, a common psychological condition that diminishes your ability to live and prosper in your personal and business relationships.

If you look back at the preceding questions, you'll notice a common thread. Every question involves two crucial elements: discomfort and other people. Simply put, social anxiety is feeling uncomfortable around other people. Social anxiety isn't clinical shyness. It is perhaps the world's most common emotional problem. And it is treatable. With your efforts this book can help you to manage these feelings.

WHAT CAUSES SOCIAL ANXIETY?

It may seem obvious that if you're uncomfortable around other people, then other people must be the cause of your discomfort. But look back at the questions that opened this chapter.

"Do you often have difficulty . . ." "When you find yourself . . ." "Do you feel tense . . ." The questions offer a clue: The cause of social anxiety is not other people, but your discomfort with yourself.

Once you discover the cause of your anxiety, you've taken the first step in overcoming your symptoms and learning to live with ease.

Even though social anxiety can feel terrible, it's really a helpful message from your psychological control center, one that invites you to pay attention to yourself. Just as your body senses heat when you get too close to a fire, social discomfort alerts you to your own negative attitudes. If you pay attention to the painful message of anxiety, you give yourself an opportunity to grow. Or, you can ignore the message and continue to feel the pain.

THE PAIN OF SOCIAL ANXIETY

If you've ever met someone important, or applied for a new job, or anticipated a date, only to experience physical reactions, like sweating, blushing, shaking, dizziness, palpitations, or nausea, then you know the high cost of social anxiety.

Sometimes just thinking about an uncomfortable situation can bring on the symptoms. And sometimes the most difficult situations *are* critical, such as meeting your new girlfriend's family, or entertaining your husband's boss.

Avoiding every situation that might provoke anxiety is difficult, and successfully avoiding anxiety means spending most of your time alone. Even if you choose *not* to sentence yourself to loneliness, even if you decide to bite the bullet and suffer through painful social encounters, you still may have the frustration of never feeling completely comfortable, of never expressing yourself fully.

If you're the type of person who's always giving yourself a kick in the pants, you may already know that calling yourself "stupid," or "clumsy," or "hopelessly unattractive" doesn't help." On the other hand, chastising yourself may be the only way you know to push yourself through the obstacle course of social encounters.

The price of social anxiety may be any or all of these: negative thoughts, painful feelings, inappropriate or self-defeating behavior, and uncomfortable physical symptoms.

At the time, you may not be aware of the processes going on inside. You may have a negative thought ("You idiot! Why did you just stand there like a dope?") in response to your inappropriate behavior (freezing like a statue when introduced to someone new). You may avoid looking for a new job (self-defeating behavior), because going on interviews makes you feel ill (uncomfortable physical symptoms)—and then you feel inadequate (painful emotions). All of these negative elements are symptoms of your social anxiety, and each fuels the others.

Does all this negativity mean it's hopeless?

Not at all!

In fact, understanding that the symptoms of social anxiety are interwoven actually makes it easier to get to the root of the problem. Instead of paying attention to just one aspect of the problem, you can approach it from many different angles.

UNDERSTANDING SOCIAL ANXIETY

Negative Thoughts. Because social anxiety is rooted in your thinking, a psychological approach is essential. By addressing your negative thoughts, you'll learn where they come from and how they developed. Then you'll be able to develop new attitudes and mental habits that lead to social ease.

Painful Emotions. You may not be aware of the emotional symptoms of anxiety, but perhaps you can remember feeling withdrawn, left out, lost, friendless, abandoned, scared, or even panicky.

Or you might be acutely aware of uncomfortable feelings, without knowing why you feel the way you do. When you're around certain people, you might feel childish, incompetent, foolish, or just plain invisible. After certain social events you may find yourself feeling unworthy, ashamed, vulgar, boring, or self-obsessed.

Painful emotions derive from negative thoughts. By learning how you've developed your negative thought patterns, you'll also discover the source of many of these emotions, and you'll learn how to deal with them.

When you begin to face your social anxiety, you'll probably be surprised by how much better you feel about yourself. When you honestly face your weaknesses, you'll have to recognize your strength. Self-blame will be replaced by realistic understanding and acceptance of yourself. When you know yourself in this way, you begin to develop self-esteem.

Uncomfortable Physical Symptoms and Inappropriate Behavior. The physical symptoms of anxiety can be particularly distressing, because they seem so obvious to others. Attempts to prevent, control or deny the physical, emotional, or mental symptoms of anxiety, can result in behavioral symptoms, like nervous laughter or compulsive talking, or total avoidance.

By learning relaxation techniques and behavioral exercises, you'll gain control of your physical and behavioral symptoms, while you're also working with your mental and emotional symptoms.

As you begin to understand how they interact, you'll find yourself overcoming negative patterns, while learning positive new ones. When you no longer have to worry about sweating, blushing, or shaking inside and out, you'll feel more at ease in your world.

A Success Story: Carol

Carol writes for a large newspaper in a major city. Her feature stories and essays are recognized around the world, and she regularly addresses members of national organizations who want more information about the many subjects in which she has become an expert. It's not just the details of her research that make Carol a popular speaker. She always manages to provide her audiences with a moving, human story.

Carol is the epitome of a self-assured journalist. She's poised, energetic, and appreciated by her employer, her community, and her readers for the good work she does. She likes her work, and feels good about putting so much of herself into each story. But Carol wasn't always a success.

Five years ago, she was having serious problems at the small alternative newspaper where she had been working for just a year. Even though she had received praise from the readers, she couldn't stand up to her boss's harsh criticism. She felt invisible. She was younger than he, had less experience, and she needed her job. How could she stand up to him and tell him he was wrong? Her inability to deal with the problems made her feel helpless and incompetent. Then Carol was asked by the local medical association to speak about her recent series of feature articles on the homeless.

She accepted, mainly because she didn't know how to say "no" politely. Then she worried. She wrote and rewrote her speech. In her head she practiced calling to cancel, telling the doctors to get someone else. She felt like a fraud. She was afraid she'd make a mistake, and they'd know she was stupid. It would prove that her boss was right.

The night of the speech, Carol was a nervous wreck. From the moment she was greeted at the door of the ballroom, she felt her heart racing. She heard herself fidgeting with her purse, opening and shutting it. Click, click, click. But she couldn't stop.

Carol tried to make conversations with the doctors to whom she was introduced, but after one or two sentences, they fell silent. All she could think was that she looked terrible. They must think her unattractive. Maybe she was sweating and they found her offensive.

The doctor who sat next to her at dinner made some sexual remarks and touched her arm, but Carol just pretended that she didn't notice and tried to eat. Finally, she gave up and slugged down her wine, then before her speech, she ordered another glass and drank it quickly.

During her speech Carol was almost oblivious of the audience. At one point, to her horror, she realized that she was pounding the podium as she talked, like an evangelist calling sinners to repent. She lost her train of thought and hurried to finish as quickly as she could, promising herself, "Never! Never Again!"

Instead of keeping that promise, Carol decided to find out what caused the terrible feelings of anxiety that she'd experienced. She began by recording similar incidents in a journal and getting in touch with the thoughts and emotions she had experienced at that time.

First, she discovered that her anxiety about public speaking was related to feelings of inadequacy, which were also the source of her problems at work. As she delved deeper, Carol learned that she had a fear of being exposed as a fraud, which in turn was based on a core feeling, a basic lack of confidence and self-esteem.

Instead of reminding herself of the excellent articles that were the reason for her public presentation, Carol made herself miserable worrying if other people liked the way she looked. She couldn't express her real thoughts, even to people who annoyed her, such as her critical boss or the aggressive man who had touched her at dinner.

But Carol learned. As she faced her weaknesses, she gained a real sense of self-knowledge, and with that, a new image of herself that included her strong points. She began to value and to speak up for herself.

Two years after the frightening speaking engagement, Carol left the alternative newspaper for a better-paying job at a much more prestigious paper. Carol's new boss gives her criticism, but he also appreciates the hard work she does, and he lets Carol know it.

Carol now looks forward to each opportunity she has to speak in public. Each presentation is a reminder that her work is appreciated. When she finds herself pounding on the podium, Carol can't help smiling, remembering her first public appearance. But now she knows that she's pounding the podium for emphasis because what she has to say is important.

THE SOCIAL ANXIETY EQUATION

The following equation helps us understand the dynamics of social anxiety. Using this formula, we can learn what it is about ourselves that makes us feel uncomfortable, and why certain people and situations exacerbate our discomfort.

Generic Anxiety + Situation Anxiety = Social Anxiety

Generic Anxiety
Although social anxiety includes a wide range of symptoms, they can all be reduced to a few basic perceptions about our-

selves. Usually our emotional symptoms are deep within, so they feel vague and are difficult to express. We call these disconcerting feelings *generic anxiety*.

Generic anxiety is feeling uncomfortable or dissatisfied with ourselves at the most basic level. When we cannot approve our appearance, our intelligence, and our social abilities, we feel generic anxiety. If we can't accept ourselves and feel comfortable with who we are and how we look, then we worry about how others see us.

When Carol went to her first speaking engagement at the medical association, it would have been natural for her to worry about what she was going to say. That kind of anxiety would have helped, because she would have spent time working on her speech. If Carol had tried to involve her audience in her work with the homeless, her intensity probably would have come across as dedication.

But Carol was worried about how she looked. Instead of concentrating on her reason for giving the presentation, Carol was concentrating on herself, focusing on her own nervous behavior and her physical symptoms. Instead of responding to the people she met, she worried that she might be offending them.

Carol's deep-rooted sense of insecurity about her intelligence and social skills made her vulnerable to criticism. She was unable to express her own offense at the doctor who had made sexual advances. Instead she spent the evening worrying that she would make mistakes and appear stupid.

Situation Anxiety

In *situation anxiety* a certain kind of event will bring out feelings of anxiety. In a psychological process called *displacement*, we displace our real feelings onto another person or occasion. If we feel stupid or inadequate, we assume that the person we're talking to thinks we're stupid or inadequate.

You may have heard yourself say, "Parties make me feel uncomfortable," or "My boss makes me feel stupid." In reality, it's you who makes yourself feel uncomfortable or stupid, but you've displaced the source of your feelings.

On their own, people and situations don't cause social anxiety, but the dynamics of an encounter can bring out generic anxiety. When Carol had to appear in front of a group of people she didn't know, presenting her own information to recognized professionals, her feelings about herself were put to the test. It was Carol's negative thoughts and painful feelings about herself that caused her anxiety.

You might be thinking, if only a specific situation triggers this anxiety, then why not concentrate on the situation? Why worry about all these generic anxiety problems that sound so much more complex and difficult to resolve?

In fact, many techniques for dealing with specific situations can be very effective. You can learn how to comfortably meet strangers, or you can learn to flirt at parties, or you can learn to assert yourself with your boss or your domineering friend. But learning these specific skills may be of little help when you find yourself in a similar, or even disparate, situation that triggers the same anxiety all over again.

The problem with confronting anxiety only in specific situations is that you avoid the problem within yourself. If you don't know how you feel about yourself, how can you be sure that a specific technique is really helping you and not just prolonging your suffering?

It was not the speaking engagement that caused Carol's feelings, but it *was* the speaking engagement that brought these feelings to the surface. Carol recognized her need to deal with the anxiety, not just to avoid all similar situations. Because she learned to deal with the problems that came up during a speaking engagement, Carol gained knowledge about herself that helped her improve other aspects of her life.

AVOIDING SOCIAL ANXIETY

Many people manage their lives by avoiding the people and situations that bring out their anxiety. But avoiding social anxiety doesn't make it go away. In fact, avoidance behavior can make anxiety worse. On top of the negative thoughts and feelings we already have, we add bad feelings about our need to avoid certain people and situations. The result is that we're left feeling unable to confront life's challenges in many different areas.

But What If I'm Shy?

When Carol first started dealing with her anxiety, she considered herself to be shy. But shyness is a behavior, not a feeling, and certainly not an unchangeable aspect of a personality. By shying away from the people and situations that trigger our feelings of anxiety, we avoid facing what is almost always the real problem: feelings of inferiority.

Shyness doesn't make you feel uncomfortable at a party or at a business meeting. Shyness doesn't cause your anxiety when you're getting ready for a date. Shyness is the way you act, because you don't want to face the reasons for the anxiety you feel.

Shyness can become an excuse for avoiding life. When we avoid the people and situations that provoke anxiety, we avoid the good parts of life as well. We begin making assumptions about what we would and would not enjoy, and we give away our chance to experience the spontaneity, the fun, and the fulfillment of life's special moments.

If we ignore the message of social anxiety, the consequences can be bleak. Marriages and families can fall apart over the inability to communicate. Jobs and career plans can falter over the inability to develop good relationships with co-workers. Friends can interpret our social discomfort as snobbishness and avoid us.

Is avoiding anxiety worth missing your own life?

Facing the truth about social anxiety shouldn't feel like the end of the world. In fact, learning that you have social anxiety can be the beginning of a new and more enjoyable life.

Carol's anxiety about her first speaking engagement gave her the momentum to work on herself. It was difficult at first, as she tried to understand herself and the roots of her anxiety.

But gradually, as her thoughts and feelings about herself improved, her relationships with other people began to reflect her positive changes.

YOUR SOCIAL ANXIETY INVENTORY

The following inventory is a tool for getting in touch with your personal set of social anxiety issues. After answering the questions below, you'll have a better idea of how social anxiety affects your life. You'll also learn what role it plays in your everyday decision-making and your long-term planning.

Answer each question as honestly as possible. Base your answers on *how you feel now, or how you usually feel*. Don't try to guess how you *should* feel, and don't answer how you'd *like* to feel. If you aren't sure of an answer skip the question and come back to it later.

If a question deals with a particular situation that you haven't experienced, or addresses some issue that doesn't involve you, skip it, or put down what you honestly think you would feel or do if you were facing that situation.

Keep your answers to this and later inventories. Upcoming exercises and techniques for reducing anxiety will use your answers from this inventory and from inventories you'll find in later chapters.

As you read through the book and become familiar with its exercises and techniques, you may want to take this inventory again. By comparing your initial responses with later scores, you'll be able to measure the progress you're making.

THE SOCIAL ANXIETY INVENTORY

Rating Scale: Answer the questions below.
Write the number of the response that best describes how you really feel in each of those situations. Then add the numbers for a total score.

0 = Comfortable, or only slight feelings of anxiety
1 = Definite feelings and symptoms of anxiety
2 = Very anxious and uncomfortable
3 = Totally incapacitated by anxiety

When I:		I Feel:		
Invite people to my house for dinner	0	1	2	3
Go to a friend's house for dinner	0	1	2	3
Have my family over to my house for dinner	0	1	2	3
Go to a family dinner hosted by my parents, or by my brothers or sisters	0	1	2	3
Am the guest of honor at a surprise party	0	1	2	3
Attend a party with some friends and some other people I don't know	0	1	2	3
Attend a dinner with people I don't know	0	1	2	3
Attend a dinner meeting with people from work	0	1	2	3
Sit down to eat lunch with people I don't know	0	1	2	3
Eat in a restaurant alone	0	1	2	3

Go out to dinner with a date, or someone I'd like to date	0	1	2	3
Want to go out with someone I've just met	0	1	2	3
Go on a date with someone I don't know, or barely know	0	1	2	3
Call someone the first time to ask for a date	0	1	2	3
Call someone I've gone out with to ask for another date	0	1	2	3
Think about what we'll do after we finish dinner	0	1	2	3
Know my date is interested in sex, but I'm not ready	0	1	2	3
Am interested in having sex, but I don't think my date is interested	0	1	2	3
Think the relationship is ready for sex, but we haven't talked about birth control	0	1	2	3
Think my loved one is getting ready to bring up a problem related to our sex life	0	1	2	3

Have to bring up
money matters with my
spouse/lover/
roommate/child   0   1   2   3

Order a meal in a
special restaurant my
date selected   0   1   2   3

Have to send my meal
back, because it's not
what I ordered   0   1   2   3

Have to tell the waiter
that the bill is incorrect   0   1   2   3

Have to confront a
friend/relative who has
let me down   0   1   2   3

Have to tell the
mechanic that my car
still doesn't work, even
though it's supposed to
be fixed   0   1   2   3

Ask my doctor to
explain what's wrong
with me   0   1   2   3

Ask a teacher to
explain my grade on a
paper   0   1   2   3

Am asked to answer a
question in front of the
class or a group of
coworkers   0   1   2   3

Need to pick out
something to wear for
a special occasion   0   1   2   3

Want to tell my hairdresser to try something different	0	1	2	3
Introduce myself to people I don't know	0	1	2	3
Meet a stranger who begins a conversation with me	0	1	2	3
Have to make a presentation in class or at work	0	1	2	3
Have an opportunity to speak in front of a large group	0	1	2	3
Should be up for a promotion, but my boss hasn't mentioned it	0	1	2	3
Decide to get a new job, which means going on interviews	0	1	2	3
Get an offer to call on someone to pursue job possibilities	0	1	2	3
Receive extra attention for doing a good job	0	1	2	3
Want someone to consider me for the job they're filling	0	1	2	3
Am representing my company at an important meeting	0	1	2	3

Meet someone who's a
leader in my field of
work   0   1   2   3

Am asked to work over
the weekend, and I've
already made special
plans   0   1   2   3

EVALUATING THE INVENTORY

0 To 10

If your score is less than ten and none of your answers is a three
consider yourself an inspiration to others! For you, a difficult
person or situation is viewed as a challenge, not as an obstacle.
Because you have learned to manage your anxiety, any mild
feelings of discomfort or tension just give you an attractive energy, often called "that special edge." Reading this book
should give you an even greater awareness of the positive attitude you already possess.

11 To 30

Congratulations! You're right to consider yourself generally at
ease, because you've learned to take your feelings of anxiety in
stride. You will probably want to use this book to focus on one
specific aspect of your life that still feels uncomfortable or difficult. Even though you're still working on your own anxiety,
don't be afraid to offer help to others.

31 To 65

Like most people, you have definite feelings of social anxiety,
but you can usually go for weeks or months, avoiding the people and situations that provoke your symptoms. You've learned
to function in spite of your discomfort, but you can't deny that
some people and some situations make you very uncomfortable. You can use the exercises in this book to help you deal
with specific people and situations, and you'll also gain a
greater awareness of yourself.

66 To 90

Many people experience a moderate level of anxiety almost all the time. You may be very uncomfortable in only a few situations, or you may feel mildly nervous under several different circumstances. If you're willing to work through the exercises in this book, seriously and consistently, you'll notice a much greater sense of social ease. Part of the change will be an increase in your self-esteem.

91 To 129

You might consider yourself to be extremely shy, because you're always avoiding people and situations that provoke your anxiety. Social anxiety prevents you from enjoying your work and having close relationships with other people. The physical and emotional symptoms of anxiety cause you to avoid people and situations that make you intensely uncomfortable. If you work on each exercise in this book, you'll be surprised at how much more comfortable you feel in your daily life. You may want to seek extra help from a counsellor or therapist.

SOCIAL ANXIETY CHART

Level 1	Level 2	Level 3	Level 4	Level 5
Minimal Anxiety	Slight Discomfort	Moderate Nervousness	Frequent Discomfort	Severe Anxiety
Inventory Evaluation Comparisons				
0 to 10	11 to 30	31 to 65	66 to 90	91 to 129
(Robbie)	(Rick)	(Molly)	(Carol)	(Don)

The dotted line at the top of the social anxiety chart shows the various levels and social anxiety reflected in the social anxiety inventory. Notice that the categories have a great deal of overlap. If your symptoms don't exactly match your ranking, you might still recognize yourself in the following descriptions of other people who completed the inventory.

Social Anxiety: Don

Don scored 108 on the inventory. Most of Don's life revolved around the anxiety he felt every day at work. He thought of himself as passive and timid; the people he worked with considered him aloof and unresponsive. Don's anxiety made it difficult for him to work effectively with the others in his department. He felt inhibited when he had to ask for help, he was afraid of criticism, and he never seemed to hear the compliments when he did a good job. After Don was passed over for a promotion, his supervisor explained that Don seemed unfriendly and disagreeable. His boss had noticed such little things as his eating lunch alone every day.

If you're at Don's end of the anxiety chart, you can make some fairly dramatic changes early on. Even though losing the promotion was a severe blow to Don, it helped him see how others perceived him. Despite his fears, he managed to work on his communication problems. First, he had to acknowledge his feelings. Then he learned to open himself enough to share them with others.

Instead of rejecting him, the people from work became open and accepting, which gave Don's self-esteem the boost he needed. He bought new clothes and smiled more. He redecorated his apartment and invited some of his new friends over for dinner. And when they returned the invitation, Don joined them for dinner and, to his own surprise, enjoyed himself!

You remember Carol's story. Five years ago, Carol scored 75 on the inventory. At the time all she could think of was learning how to protect herself from ever repeating that one frightening speaking engagement. But Carol quickly realized that deeper problems were at work. She began to deal with her sense of inadequacy and the difficulty she had expressing herself to other people. She learned to replace her negative thoughts with more realistic ones. Carol noticed small changes in herself immediately, and within two years, she turned her life around.

Moderate Nervousness: Molly

Molly is a physician. For the first few years after she began her practice, she felt content and satisfied. She was warm and caring with her patients, relaxed with her support staff, and happy with her small group of close friends. But when she began to attend functions with large groups of people she didn't know, she recognized growing level of discomfort. When members of a women's group asked Molly to speak, she accepted, but found the experience unnerving. Her hands shook so badly that she could barely read the speech she'd prepared. Her score on the inventory was 42.

Molly's moderate level of nervousness could be avoided if she were willing to avoid new people and new situations. But like many people, she did not want to miss out on new opportunities in her life and career. Dealing with her anxiety meant facing and exploring the vague feelings of discomfort that she felt in strange circumstances.

Although accomplished and self-sufficient in some aspects of life, Molly had never dealt with her insecurity about her appearance. Her doctor's smock kept her body hidden much of the time, and she avoided mirrors whenever she could. Being in the public eye made Molly acknowledge that she had refused to deal with a painful issue.

She hadn't paid attention to her appearance during her busy years in college and medical school, in fact, had no experience with such things. She decided to visit a professional grooming advisor. She learned where to get a better haircut and how to apply makeup. She decided to take the time for an occasional manicure. She learned to recognize colors that made her look and feel good, and she learned to dress in a style that was comfortable, but also flattering.

Molly's efforts didn't go without notice. She received compliments after speaking to local parenting groups, and began to make valuable professional, and even romantic contacts.

Slight Discomfort: Rick

Rick works in an advertising agency. He is friendly and humorous, often sharing ancedotes about his wild romantic adventures with the people at work. Everyone in the agency seems to know and like Rick, and they count on him to energize meetings and parties. But Rick has a problem no one knows about. Instead of moving into a supervisory position that he's easily qualified for, he holds himself back, because he's afraid to give criticism. When he decided to work on this particular fear, Rick took the inventory and scored 18.

Rick began to see that a large part of his life was frustrated by his secret anxiety. He began to keep a record of his negative thoughts and feelings. From his journal work, Rick learned that his inability to criticize others came from a deeper fear of being rejected. As long as he was always making others laugh, he didn't have to worry that they would like him.

Minimal Anxiety: Robbie

Robbie is a professional football player who appears often on television. He and his wife were excited to start a family, and the baby's arrival was a thrill for them. Robbie found his baby daughter fascinating; he spent hours just watching her. But when anyone else was around, including his wife, he felt inhibited and uncomfortable. He was embarrassed to be seen as a gentle, nurturing person, yet his new relationship with his daughter was also important to him. Robbie talked to a friend about his problem, and took the social anxiety inventory. He scored 9.

Robbie is one of the fortunate few who always seem to be at ease, but appearances can be deceiving. The birth of his daughter awakened tender feelings that he didn't know he had. Although he felt confused by the situation at first, Robbie found that working on mental and emotional exercises helped him understand his new feelings. Gradually, he learned to accept the parts of himself that had been pushed aside by the outgoing, boisterous personality he showed the world.

The change in Robbie was a surprise to his wife; she had worried how Robbie would react to having a daughter instead of a son. As Robbie became more comfortable being with his baby in public, he began to take much more responsibility for her care.

When Robbie took his daughter to football practice for the first time, he created a stir. He thoroughly enjoyed himself as forty grown men filed by to talk baby talk to his daughter.

EMBARKATION ORDERS

The journey of becoming at ease with others is really a journey of becoming at ease with ourselves. No task is more exciting, challenging, or fulfilling than the effort to become a more aware, complete person. Whether your social anxiety is a minor annoyance or a pervasive feeling that provokes a constant inner struggle, you can learn to become more at ease.

Each chapter in this book will help you better understand your response to the people and situations in your life. You'll uncover the thoughts and emotions that provoke your anxiety, and you'll learn to change those negative patterns into realistic ones. Once you know your real self, you'll learn to express your thoughts and feelings to the people around you.

You'll learn how generic anxiety can affect your everyday interactions with people, and you'll learn how to deal with difficult physical and behavioral symptoms. Perhaps most helpful of all, you'll change your reality by using the power you have within yourself: your imagination. You'll learn to use relaxation and visualization techniques to gain a sense of ease, with yourself and with other people. You'll learn how to approach some of the most difficult situations you face in your work and your personal life.

Once you've decided to make the journey to realize your authentic self, commit yourself to the time and effort it takes. Feel free to skip ahead in the book if a particular subject interests you, but allow yourself to really participate by answering all the questions and completing every exercise. Your reward will be the joy you experience as your self-esteem begins to flourish.

2 EASING YOUR MIND

Anxiety comes from not being able to know the world you're in, not being able to orient yourself in your own existence . . .

ROLLO MAY

Most people are unaware of their own thinking much of the time. Most people are also out of touch with many of their own feelings. Observing and analyzing our thoughts and feelings is something few of us do on a regular basis.

When things go awry, we might feel bad, or irritable, but we usually accept feeling bad as a necessary part of life. Even people who are aware that bad feelings can be caused by "bad thinking" don't try to change their thoughts. But altering the way we think can actually change the way we feel.

THE COGNITIVE CONNECTION

Psychologists and psychiatrists have studied the connection between thoughts and feelings for many years. The conclusions of two pioneers in this field, Aaron T. Beck, M.D. and Dr. Albert Ellis, Ph.D. are described in depth in two helpful books. *Feeling Good: The New Mood Therapy* by David Burns,

M.D. and *Healing the Shame That Binds You* by John Bradshaw, a counselor and theologian.

Over several years of studying patients, Drs. Beck and Ellis noticed that thoughts could generate feelings. They call this mental-emotional connection the *cognitive theory*. Cognitive therapists are those who help patients with their emotions by addressing the way they think.

We have thousands and thousands of thoughts, some originating in infancy and childhood, others derived from more recent experiences. Some are thoughts we've analyzed, thoughts of which we're cognizant; others we've accepted without conscious awareness.

Some of the thoughts that underlie our most basic feelings about ourselves come to us from other people. All too often, we've never stopped to question their validity.

If your high school teacher said that you were incapable of learning, you might have believed it and quit reading books. If your parent said, "You're a lazy bum!" you might have accepted that as true, stopped trying, and *become* a lazy bum. Or you might be working too hard twenty years later, still trying to prove that parent wrong.

When how we think about ourselves becomes automatic, we can get stuck with behavior and emotions that may not be what we truly want from life. The self-fulfilling prophecy is one result.

Automatic Thinking: Bill

Bill and Joanna were going to spend a year in Mexico, so they decided to take a refresher course in Spanish. Joanna felt excited about the class. "This will be fun," she told herself. "I enjoy challenges." Bill forced himself to sign up, but he dreaded every minute. "Why bother?" he told himself before each class. "I was never any good at languages."

No one would be surprised to learn that Joanna did far better in the class than Bill, but what may surprise you is what happened in Mexico.

After a few miserable, self-conscious weeks, Bill met some men who invited him to go deep-sea fishing, something he'd always wanted to do. Bill was nervous about going; the men spoke little English, and he felt awkward and stupid trying to speak Spanish. But he couldn't pass up the fishing trip! The other men encouraged him to speak Spanish as they knew little English. He had a wonderful time. Soon, Bill found himself speaking fluently with everyone he met. Joanna was amazed by Bill's ability. During most of their stay she let him do the talking for her.

When he took the Spanish class Bill was unaware that he had accepted a negative thought about himself; the idea that he was no good at languages. If he'd analyzed his thinking, he might have realized that he never really had had a chance to speak and interact with people in another language. He should have given himself more of a chance.

Fortunately for Bill the acceptance he found on the fishing trip overrode his self-criticism enough that he could attempt conversation. Many of us haven't been as lucky. Our inner messages prevent us from putting ourselves into a new situation where others might give us the encouragement we need.

CHANGING YOUR THINKING

It's our own *thinking,* not other people or specific situations, that make us uncomfortable. The approval we really need is our own. Other people can't mold our thinking unless we allow them to.

Imagine what would have happened if you had been able to speak up for yourself when you were still young. Think how differently you might feel now if you'd answered that teacher who accused you of not being able to learn.

"No, Mrs. Jones," you might have said. "I can learn when the material is presented in a logical, interesting way. To tell you the truth, I'm just bored." You might have annoyed the teacher, but at least you wouldn't have accepted a negative, untrue thought about yourself.

When we accept negative statements about ourselves, it's usually because we're not aware of our own thoughts—about ourselves, about the other people involved, and about the particular situation. Unless we are aware of our thoughts, it's difficult to change them.

This is why cognitive therapy is useful. It provides tools to help us become more aware of our thoughts and feelings. The social anxiety inventory, journal exercises, and visualization exercises in this book are cognitive therapy tools. By learning to evaluate our thoughts, we can unearth the negative and unrealistic patterns that cause our anxious feelings and behavior.

DISTORTED THOUGHT PATTERNS

It's a healthy human characteristic to be influenced by messages from the subconscious; if we were wholly aware of every single aspect of our thinking, daily life would be impossibly cumbersome. But when our thoughts are conscious, we have the ability to evaluate them and to accept or reject them.

When we automatically accept negative and self-defeating thoughts as being realistic and true, they become part of our unconscious image of ourselves. Negative thoughts contain many different types of distortions, including exaggerations, generalizations, and illogical assumptions. Yet these distortions can be so insidious that we are totally unaware of them until we react to them with nervousness and anxiety.

To exercise our powers of analysis and rejection, we need to learn the most common patterns of distorted thinking. Then we will be aware when our own patterns are similarly distorted and cause anxiety.

As you read the descriptions of the seven most common thought distortions, try to assess your own patterns. Do any of the distortions seem familiar?

SEVEN PATTERNS OF DISTORTED THINKING

1. *Generalizing.* When you generalize, you make a global conclusion based on one specific incident. One action, or one failure to act, one error, or one negative feeling and you assign yourself the permanent label of "jerk," or "wimp," or "failure."

Another way to generalize is to use the universal qualifiers: always, never, no one, everybody. "No one will ever like me," you think after one disappointment. When a date turns out to be less than marvelous, you tell yourself, "I'll always be a loser at love."

When you generalize, you tend to make absolute assumptions based on insufficient evidence: "I didn't do well in this interview, so I better give up my idea of getting a new job. I guess I'm stuck in this job forever."

When you combine generalizations, you can jump from, "She didn't want to go out with me," to "No one will ever like me." Then you label yourself: "I'm a social Neanderthal."

2. *Predicting the Future.* This is what you do when you anticipate what's going to happen an hour from now, or tomorrow, or next year. And you'll usually be imagining the worst possible outcome.

Maybe you sound like this, "I'd like to go to that dinner party, but I know no one will talk to me. Then I'll feel uncomfortable. I'll make a fool of myself, and everyone will laugh. I'd better stay home."

With this kind of fortune-telling ability, you never can allow yourself to make mistakes, because *you should have known better.*

You rationalize your predictions by telling yourself you're being realistic. You only want to be prepared for whatever will happen. But you can't possibly predict a positive outcome for yourself and risk disappointment.

Since the future you predict is always the worst of all possible worlds, how can you help but feel anxious? Wouldn't any reasonable person want to avoid the horrors you imagine?

3. *Mind Reading.* Now it's not just your own future you can see. You know what's going on in other people's minds. And guess what? It's always something negative about *you.* From, "Sue didn't ask me to go to lunch with her," you determine "She obviously doesn't want to be friends with me."

Mind reading, predicting the future, and generalizing can often work together, creating a confusing downward spiral of negative thought distortions. You might start with a simple bit of sad reality: "Josh didn't ask me to his party." But soon you're mind reading. "He'll never want to go out with me." Next you generalize, labeling yourself by saying, "I'm a social misfit." And before long, you're predicting the future: "I'll always be alone."

4. *Dwelling on the Past.* This negative pattern gives you a chance to memorialize every negative experience. You might tell yourself that it's a sign of maturity to learn from your mistakes, but instead of progressing, you're programming yourself for another failure.

If you ended an unhappy marriage, the lesson you took away might be: "My marriage was a failure; I'll never be able to find a good mate." If you felt anxious at a business meeting, you might tell yourself "I was self-conscious at the last meeting. I probably shouldn't go again."

Another method of dwelling on the past is couching your negative experiences in terms of your inability to change. "If only my parents had been better communicators," you think, blaming your parents and your childhood for your current problems, instead of trying to help yourself.

5. *You Must/You Should.* A particularly self-defeating pattern, you must/you should thinking is like a system of rules based on ideals that have nothing to do with who you are or what you want in life.

"I have to speak at the church dinner next month," you tell yourself, even though you dread the idea. Instead of dealing with your feelings of anxiety, you tell yourself, "Everyone else has spoken, and I have to do my part."

You're probably not aware that you've become the victim of arbitrary rules, instead of the active creator of your own choices. You give yourself mental kicks to control your emotional and physical symptoms of anxiety.

When asked to join a breakfast group, you swallow your anxiety and accept, telling yourself, "I should be able to handle this!" Then you chastise yourself, throwing in some generalizations: "No one should feel so nervous about going to a meeting once a month. Don't be such a wimp!"

6. *Win or Lose.* The ultimate in negative thought patterns, win or lose thinking means you demand perfection—always. With this rigid mind-set, you can't allow compromises.

If you feel anxious about going to a new restaurant, then the whole evening is ruined. If someone isn't particularly nice to you, watch out! That person becomes an instant enemy. Anyone who doesn't agree with you is against you. Either your new relationship is total bliss, or it's not working. Your new job must be a total success, or it's an utter disaster.

7. *Twisted Logic.* No matter what happens, you can turn it into a negative conclusion about yourself. Twisted logic isn't logical. "If Ben thought I was attractive," you think, "he would have asked me out." And then you conclude, "I must not be attractive."

Twisted logic doesn't make sense. You just heard about an affordable new apartment with lots of windows, close to your work. But it's a single, and now you have to tell your current roommates. You think, "What if they're mad that I'm moving out?" Then you worry, "What if they don't care?"

You can get so twisted that you worry about polar opposites. You're meeting a new client, and you think, "What if they hate my work?" At the same time you worry, "What if I get the account and then I can't deliver?" Or you're going out with someone you just met and find yourself thinking, "What if he doesn't like me? Or what if he likes me too much?"

OWNING YOUR THOUGHTS

Maybe you feel even more hopeless now that you know the many patterns of distorted thinking to which you're susceptible. Maybe your thoughts and feelings still seem inaccessible. Maybe you worry that you'll have to resort to years of psycho-analysis to unravel the negative jumble in your head.

Believe it or not, you've already learned enough to evaluate your own thoughts. And it's a process you can do on your own. With a little practice, mental self-awareness and evaluation will become natural to you.

The more familiar you become with your own patterns of distorted thinking, the easier it will be to sort out your self-defeating thoughts and see yourself from a realistic perspective. Owning your thoughts means dealing with the source of your anxious feelings and behavior.

Taking responsibility for your own thoughts is essential for easing anxiety. When your negative thoughts have less control over your feelings, your social anxiety will also begin to decrease.

THE JOURNAL PROCESS

Dealing with the distorted thoughts that cause anxiety may not be easy at first. Sometimes it's hard to know what you're thinking and feeling, and it's always difficult to remember specific thoughts and feelings after a long period of time. One method that will help you approach your thoughts and feelings is writing in a journal.

Writing your thoughts and feelings down is the best way to get in touch with yourself and monitor your changes over time. Writing in a journal gives you a record of your progress as you confront your anxiety. To help you start, this book includes journal exercises that deal with each successive step in learning to live with ease.

A journal is a private form of self-expression. It's important to remember that no one need read it but you. No one else even needs to know about it.

In a journal, you can write whatever you want, however you want, whenever you want. You don't have to follow any rules or conform to any style. Using a journal is like opening a window into your psyche. You peer into yourself, and your thoughts, feelings, and memories come out on the page.

Using a journal is not a new technique. For centuries people have kept journals and diaries to record events in their lives, to keep track of the passage of time, and to monitor their own progress and personal development. Many journals that have survived belonged to novelists, poets, and painters—people involved in creative and mental struggles, who needed a source for self-exploration.

By writing in journals, we get to know ourselves. "I wish I could be more adaptable and live more gaily in the present world," wrote Lady Murasaki, an eleventh-century Japanese writer, and perhaps the world's first novelist.

Henry David Thoreau, the transcendentalist writer, became famous for his notes on nature. Writing specialist Elizabeth Irvin Ross has noted that Thoreau also chronicled his personal growth in a journal, as he changed from, "a parcel of vain strivings held by a chance bond together," into the self-directed writer of *Walden Pond.*

In *The New Diary,* Tristine Rainer suggests that writing in a journal is the only form of writing that encourages total freedom of expression.

Your Own Journal
Your journal is going to play a special role in helping you overcome your anxiety so you may want to get a special book, something you won't use for any other purpose. Save your journal for your thoughts about yourself, not for grocery lists, letters, or daily reminders. Think of your journal as a tool that helps you understand and lessen your anxiety.

You can use any kind of book you like. Your journal can be a large drawing pad, a pocket-sized notebook, a spiral or three-ring notebook or a hardbound book of blank pages. Make your journal special and appealing so you'll want to use it. And keep it with you. Writing in your journal is going to become an important part of your life!

Your Journal Exercises
Your goal is to write spontaneously, whenever you have something to write, wherever you are, whatever thoughts or feelings come to you. Don't worry if you find it difficult getting started. The journal exercises in each chapter will help you begin to know yourself through writing.

JOURNAL EXERCISE #1

This exercise is to help you get in touch with your own thinking. Try not to edit or criticize your thoughts, just record whatever comes into your head. Be as specific as you can.

1. Begin by carrying your journal with you. For one entire day, keep track of every emotion you feel and whatever thoughts go with each feeling. For example, if a negative feeling comes up, whatever it is, write it down. If you feel anxious, lonely, or even panicked, write that down. Then try to focus on what you're thinking, and write that down, too.

2. When you are finished, look for patterns in what you have written. Recognizing the patterns will help you gain insights.

Jim is a part-time actor with a successful business as a vocal coach and piano instructor. On his first day of keeping his journal, Jim was called for an audition. Here's a sample page from his journal.

JIM'S JOURNAL

Feelings: Fear, Panic.

Thoughts: I haven't been on an audition for months! I'm not prepared! They sure don't want me for my looks; I'm too old to worry about that. I didn't get jobs twenty years ago when I looked good, so what chance have I got now? Wait till I tell them my last role was two years ago in a commercial. Why even take the time to go? These people want winners, not losers.

Jim's thoughts show some clearly distorted patterns. He's dwelling on the past and generalizing, by labeling himself a loser. Do you recognize any of these distorted patterns in your thinking?

You may have noticed that Jim's feelings of fear and panic were accompanied by very specific thoughts. If you find it difficult to identify your feelings at first, try to notice when your mood shifts. Then write down your thoughts about whatever is happening at that moment. Although your feelings may still be vague, you might be able to pinpoint what you're feeling by focusing on your thoughts.

YOUR FREEDOM TO CHOOSE

When you begin examining your thoughts and feelings, it's natural to wonder if what you think is rational and to question whether your feelings are appropriate. It's not always easy to determine what is appropriate and rational, but as you learn to evaluate your thoughts and feelings in terms of what is happening in your life, you'll begin to distinguish your actual feelings and thoughts from your expectations. And you'll begin to exercise your freedom to choose your own meanings about your life.

For example, if you're facing surgery, you may feel scared and anxious. But you may also be looking forward to the relief from pain the operation promises. If you've just had an important relationship dissolve, it's appropriate to feel sad and lonely. But you might also be enjoying your new-found independence.

You'll find that it's sometimes appropriate to be upset with yourself. When you're not sure whether it's okay to be upset, ask yourself if your feelings are in proportion to the situation.

If you lock your keys in your car, you may feel a little disturbed by your forgetfulness. You may say:

> "Damn! I knew I shouldn't have put the keys on the seat when I put those packages in the care! That was pretty stupid. Now, I'm going to have to call a locksmith, and I'm going to be late getting home, and we're going out to dinner. My wife is going to be irritated. I'd better call her."

You're feeling frustrated, and self-critical, but these feelings are understandable, given the circumstances. But if you say:

> "Damn! I did it again! This is the third time I've locked myself out of the car! No matter what car I have, I manage to lock myself out of it. My wife is going to kill me. I'm going to make us late to the restaurant, and everyone will be furious! Maybe I should just call and tell them to go without me. I can't believe I'm so stupid. I'll never try to go shopping on my way home, again. Something like this is bound to happen."

In this case, you're not dealing with the specific situation. You're generalizing and dwelling on the past. Instead of accepting responsibility, you allowed the incident to spark a recital of every similar mistake you've ever made, with some grandiose conclusions added as punishment.

It can be appropriate to be upset with yourself, but it's never appropriate to inflict your negative thoughts on others. If you try to blame your mistake on someone else or displace your feelings onto the situation, your negative response will become contagious, and you'll be adding more frustrations to the ones you already have.

Self-limited anger is healthy. Once you express your anger at your behavior, your mood of irritation lifts. You solve the problem, and get back on track. Sure, calling the locksmith will take time, but if you call your wife and explain the situation, there's no reason you can't meet your friends for the evening.

But when you begin to follow a self-deafeating thought pattern, you soon wind up in a maze of conflicting negative statements. Instead of dealing with the problem at hand, your energy goes into self-criticism. A small problem turns into a trap door, leading to anxiety.

JOURNAL EXERCISE #2

This exercise will help you tune in to your everyday thoughts and feelings. As you become more familiar with your usual mental and emotional states, you'll be able to distinguish self-defeating patterns that create anxiety.

1. For one week write down what you feel at regular times each day: when you get up, when you eat lunch, when you come home, and when you're getting ready for bed. Write down whatever your thoughts are at these times, without editing yourself.

2. Each day, go back and look at what you wrote the day before. Are your thoughts and feelings getting easier to recognize? Have you noticed any distortions in your thinking?

3. As you go over your notes from the previous day or week, make additional notes about anything that now seems unclear. If something you wrote yesterday now

seems confusing, you might write, "What did this mean?" or "This doesn't make sense!" Feel free to add commentary: "How revealing!" or, "Do I sound like I've got a grudge!"

WHAT ARE YOU AFRAID OF?

If you've been avoiding the journal exercises, ask yourself why. What do you think will happen if you write down your thoughts and feelings? Maybe you've been telling yourself that writing all this stuff down is silly. You might think you don't need to pay attention to your emotions and thoughts, or maybe you believe you can just think about the exercises and get the same result.

It's not that simple. If you could attain self-knowledge simply by thinking about your anxiety, you already would have learned everything there is to know about yourself. If you really want to learn how to manage your anxiety, you'll find that the time it takes to discover who is really inside you is worth every bit of the effort.

If part of you is afraid of being exposed, that side of you will come up with every excuse imaginable *not to do the exercises.* Ask yourself, "What am I afraid of?" and listen for the voice of resistance. Keep asking yourself the same question until you get an answer.

BREAKING YOUR RESISTANCE

When it's difficult to make yourself write in your journal, try one of these resistance-breaking techniques.

1. You might feel inhibited about writing. You might not feel "creative" enough, or sufficiently "literary." That's not the purpose. Don't think of yourself as a creative

writer. Think of yourself as a recorder or an investigative reporter. It's your job to write down every thought and feeling that comes into your brain. Get down all the words, including the "umm's," the "you know's," and the pauses in your thoughts. If a word escapes you, leave a blank space.

In fact, be as uncreative as possible. No glowing adjectives, no perfect sentence structures, no embellishments, no judgments.

2. Maybe the idea of writing in a book or a notebook is inhibiting. You might have illegible handwriting, or maybe your hand cramps. Don't be stopped by that. Find the instrument that is right for you. If using a typewriter is easier, there's no reason you can't type your journal work. If you use a computer, you can print each entry as soon as you finish writing it, then put it in your notebook.

Maybe the act of writing is the problem. You might try recording your thoughts and feelings into a tape recorder. Talking to yourself can be very liberating, and it's a fast way to record what's in your mind. But don't avoid the second step. Transcribe the tape so you can put each entry in your notebook at the end of the day. You'll want to be able to review it later.

3. If you're having trouble getting in touch with your thoughts, then write down your nonthoughts. "I'm not thinking anything," is a good place to start, or, "My mind is blank." Keep writing down whatever comes into your head.

4. Recording your thoughts at regular intervals during the day may be easy for you, but what if you find it difficult or impossible even to guess what you're feeling. Maybe you don't feel anything. That's fine. Write that down. "I feel nothing," or "I feel numb," are both good entries.

5. Keep trying.

YOUR FEELINGS INVENTORY

Knowing how you really feel is crucial in learning to deal with the emotional symptoms of anxiety. If you feel removed from your feelings, or unable to define them, the Social Anxiety Feelings Inventory below will help you. By recalling certain situations, you'll also call up the feelings you've experienced. Giving a name to your emotional experiences lets you put your anxiety into perspective.

In each part of the inventory, imagine that you are facing a social encounter. Try to bring to mind events you have actually experienced. The questions are repeated in three categories to help you assess the anxiety present in your professional life, your personal life, and your public life.

For the questions concerning your professional life, you could imagine attending an event—like a business meeting, or a party with your spouse's coworkers, or an unplanned luncheon. Or you might think about talking to someone intimidating—perhaps your boss, or an abrasive coworker.

When you think about your personal life, try remembering a family get-together, or an important meeting with your child's teacher. You might recall a difficult discussion with a significant person in your life. Or you might imagine yourself talking to someone you'd like to date.

Your public life involves any activity in which you are surrounded by strangers or people you don't know well. A public encounter could be answering a question in class, or giving a lecture to a group. Try to imagine yourself in a situation that involves people you don't know.

Before you answer each question, think about how you feel before, during, and after a similar type of encounter. Imagine the situation as vividly as possible. Try to put faces on the other people involved, and experience your feelings as if they were happening.

Answer each question as honestly as you can, using the inventory rating scale.

THE SOCIAL ANXIETY FEELINGS INVENTORY

Rating Scale: Answer the questions below, indicating how often you experience each feeling.

0 = Rarely, or never experienced
1 = Experienced at times, but not often
2 = Experienced often, but not all the time
3 = Experienced most or all of the time

At a professional social encounter, do you ever feel:

Like a child?	0	1	2	3
Intimidated?	0	1	2	3
Transparent?	0	1	2	3
Unworthy of notice?	0	1	2	3
Abandoned?	0	1	2	3
Like crying?	0	1	2	3
Preoccupied?	0	1	2	3
Aloof or withdrawn?	0	1	2	3
Self-conscious?	0	1	2	3
Lonely?	0	1	2	3
Friendless?	0	1	2	3
Resentful?	0	1	2	3
Envious?	0	1	2	3
Awkward, unsure of yourself?	0	1	2	3
Uncomfortable?	0	1	2	3

Ashamed?	0	1	2	3
Embarrassed?	0	1	2	3
Frightened or scared?	0	1	2	3
Terrified?	0	1	2	3
Panic stricken?	0	1	2	3
Vulgar or rude?	0	1	2	3
As if you're boring?	0	1	2	3
As if you'd like to escape?	0	1	2	3
As if you can't concentrate?	0	1	2	3

When you're with friends or members of your family, do you ever feel:

Like a child?	0	1	2	3
Intimidated?	0	1	2	3
Transparent?	0	1	2	3
Unworthy of notice?	0	1	2	3
Abandoned?	0	1	2	3
Like crying?	0	1	2	3
Preoccupied?	0	1	2	3
Aloof or withdrawn?	0	1	2	3
Self-conscious?	0	1	2	3
Lonely?	0	1	2	3
Friendless?	0	1	2	3
Resentful?	0	1	2	3

Envious?	0	1	2	3
Awkward or unsure of yourself?	0	1	2	3
Uncomfortable?	0	1	2	3
Ashamed?	0	1	2	3
Embarrassed?	0	1	2	3
Frightened or scared?	0	1	2	3
Terrified?	0	1	2	3
Panic stricken?	0	1	2	3
Vulgar or rude?	0	1	2	3
As if you're boring?	0	1	2	3
As if you'd like to escape?	0	1	2	3
As if you can't concentrate?	0	1	2	3

When you're with people you don't know do you ever feel:

Like a child?	0	1	2	3
Intimidated?	0	1	2	3
Transparent?	0	1	2	3
Unworthy of notice?	0	1	2	3
Abandoned?	0	1	2	3
Like crying?	0	1	2	3
Preoccupied?	0	1	2	3
Aloof or withdrawn?	0	1	2	3
Self-conscious?	0	1	2	3

Lonely?	0	1	2	3
Friendless?	0	1	2	3
Resentful?	0	1	2	3
Envious?	0	1	2	3
Awkward or unsure of yourself?	0	1	2	3
Uncomfortable?	0	1	2	3
Ashamed?	0	1	2	3
Embarrassed?	0	1	2	3
Frightened or scared?	0	1	2	3
Terrified?	0	1	2	3
Panic stricken?	0	1	2	3
Vulgar or rude?	0	1	2	3
As if you're boring?	0	1	2	3
As if you'd like to escape?	0	1	2	3
As if you can't concentrate?	0	1	2	3

USING YOUR FEELINGS INVENTORY

If you rated several questions on the inventory with 2s or 3s, don't be alarmed. Identifying your feelings and being able to recognize their different intensities means that you are becoming more aware of your emotional life. At this early stage of learning about your anxiety, the more feelings you can acknowledge, the better.

A low score is not necessarily a good score. Some people are more in touch with one aspect of their life than they are about others. A low score on one part of the inventory might be a signal for you to look more closely at a different part of your life that has been difficult to face—so difficult, in fact, that you are trying to ignore it entirely.

JOURNAL EXERCISE #3

This exercise will help you understand your responses to the Social Anxiety Feelings Inventory.

    1. Look over your inventory ratings. For any questions you rated 2 or 3, write a short description of the specific event or encounter you were thinking about as you answered the question. For example: "Being asked to give a presentation at work," or "That terrible party my husband took me to last month."

    2. As you think about your specific incident or event, try to remember exactly how you felt and what you did. Write down what the actual experience was like for you. For example, if the incident was something you actually experienced, such as being questioned unexpectedly at the last faculty meeting about a low grade you gave one of the top students, how did you feel? What did you do or say?

    Or, perhaps just anticipating a particular event or encounter created anxious feelings for you. For instance, you wanted to explain your ideas about the company's new benefits program, but you never managed to speak out. Or, perhaps you wanted to ask someone out to dinner, but you never got the nerve? If you avoided the experience, write down how you felt afterwards.

    3. If you can't remember your actual feelings about an incident, then *make them up!* Be as creative or as uncreative as you can, but write down even imaginary feelings! You may find that these so-called imaginary feelings are not too far removed from your real ones.

3 AT EASE WITH YOUR FEELINGS

To be nobody-but-myself—in world which is doing its best, night and day, to make you everybody else—means to fight the hardest battle which any human being can fight, and never stop fighting.

E. E. CUMMINGS

If a coworker asks how you are, do you answer, "fine," even if it's not what you're really feeling? If a friend asks your advice, do you share your feelings on the subject, or do you respond only with a carefully prepared opinion?

Maybe you're good at analyzing situations, but find it difficult to express your feelings. If you think you know how people expect you to feel, acknowledging that you feel differently can be difficult. Perhaps your feelings don't seem feminine enough, or perhaps they seem too feminine. Maybe you feel childish, or selfish, or incompetent, and you don't want to admit it, even to yourself.

Do you really know what your own feelings are? Can you accept being sad? Or angry? Or lonely? Maybe you don't want to admit to others what you really feel, because you're afraid that you're the only person in the world who feels that way.

Or perhaps you manage your anxiety by avoiding as many uncomfortable situations as possible, so you won't have to think about how you feel. What happens when you can't avoid an uncomfortable encounter? Do you feel out of control, trapped by external events, forced to deal with people you'd rather avoid?

THE POWER OF SELF-ESTEEM

Self-esteem encompasses our most basic feelings about ourselves: our sense of identity, our sense of self-respect, and our sense of self-worth. When we have high self-esteem, we feel comfortable with ourselves, and we don't feel as vulnerable to other people. A strong sense of self is not threatened by other people's opinions.

But when our basic feelings about ourselves are not good, we have low levels of self-esteem. Poor self-esteem is the basis for all the mental, emotional, physical, and behavioral symptoms we identify as social anxiety.

When we can admit that we feel uneasy with certain people under certain social conditions, we take the first step in dealing with social anxiety. Admitting that we are uneasy about our very feelings is the first step in improving self-esteem.

Where does low self-esteem come from? Why do some people seem to have high self-esteem and little social anxiety, while others must constantly battle nervousness and a lack of belief in themselves?

Just as negative, self-defeating thought patterns can emerge at any time in our development, so can problems with self-esteem. For many people, low self-esteem develops in childhood, when we are naturally inexperienced and vulnerable. An early insult to a child's sense of self may appear insignificant, but can have a life-long impact.

Without thinking, a parent might tell a child he's "hopeless," because at a school party the child didn't know how to talk to other children or mingle. To the parent, the incident was merely disappointing. But to the child, who vividly experiences his parent's disappointment, the incident can mark the beginning of a lifetime of social fear and avoidance.

Whenever a life experience results in feelings of failure and disappointment, whether it is our own or disappointment shown by people significant to us, any similar experience can become a test of our worth. Fearing that we might prove ourselves unworthy again, we try to avoid repeating the experience.

When we can't avoid such situations, our feelings of anxiety can seem overwhelming. But protecting our self-esteem by avoiding anxiety-provoking encounters means losing out on life's possibilities. It's not just the inevitably unpleasant interactions we give up; we also lose out on potentially meaningful, enjoyable experiences that make life worthwhile.

Sharing our true self with other human beings can be a wonderful, fulfilling experience. Increasing our knowledge and awareness of ourselves by tuning in to our feelings actually increases our sense of self-esteem. The more we know and accept ourselves, the less vulnerable we are to hurt from others.

SELF-ACCEPTANCE

"But what if I have negative feelings about myself?" you might ask. "How can I accept *them*?"

Accepting your feelings doesn't mean that you have to enjoy them. No feeling is right, and no feeling is wrong. A feeling simply is a feeling. To accept yourself means to stop fighting what you feel or don't feel and to start recognizing the validity of your own emotional life. Accepting yourself means accepting your unique emotional reactions.

Self-Acceptance: Harry
Harry is an English teacher in a large, urban high school. Every year, the faculty at Harry's school throw a picnic for the students. Harry confided to Mae, another member of the English department, that he wouldn't be able to make this year's event, because he had plans to meet an old girlfriend who was in town on a brief visit. The day of

the picnic was the only day Harry's old friend could arrange to see him.

Mae let Harry know that she was very disappointed. In the weeks before the picnic, she had made several remarks about not being able to count on Harry. Finally, Harry caved in. He called his old friend and cancelled his date. He told himself that it was important to his work that he please Mae. Conflict within the English department would make his life miserable.

On the day of the picnic, Harry felt anxious. In fact, his anxiety was so disturbing that he talked to a friend about it that evening and later spent some time writing down his feelings. Harry discovered that what he had originally considered anxiety actually involved specific feelings, including fear, resentment, and frustration. He also felt depressed, dependent, trapped, and impotent.

Harry was surprised to find that writing about his feelings revealed so much about himself. As he went over the situation in detail, Harry realized that he reacted to Mae exactly as he used to with his father, giving in to doing things he didn't want to do. Eventually, Harry discovered that caving in to his father's and Mae's demands made the immediate situations easier to deal with, but damaged his self-esteem.

Harry realized that it was his inability to accept his feelings as valid that allowed Mae to pressure him. His date with his old friend had meant a lot to him. If he had respected himself more, he might have felt entitled to respect from Mae. Instead, Harry let her feelings override his own.

Harry decided to pay more attention to his own feelings. As he learned to accept them, he realized that neither Mae nor his father *made* him feel bad about himself; it was his emotional reactions to them that brought about his negative feelings about himself.

Harry's next step was to work on his assertiveness skills, so that in the future he would not allow himself to be manipulated.

Self-Acceptance: Laura

A successful management consultant in her late 40s, Laura was recently promoted to a position for which she was not prepared. Her previous work involved analyzing others, but her critiques had always been structured and problem-oriented.

Now, as the new consultant trainer for her company, Laura had to give regular critiques of her subordinates. Her comprehensive performance reviews had to include such details as tone of voice, appearance, and behavioral manner, in addition to an assessment of each consultant's work performance.

In her new position, Laura found herself incapacitated by anxiety. Even though she could clearly see that several new consultants needed help, she couldn't bring herself to hurt or embarrass them with her critiques, which meant that she was doing an inadequate job as a trainer.

Laura knew she had to do something about her anxiety. It was making her work impossible. Because her problem was so crucial and so immediate, she decided to talk with a therapist.

The first step for Laura was to become aware of her feelings, not only about her work, but about other aspects of her life. She was eager to begin, but what she found surprised her.

Laura was asked, "How do you feel about your promotion?" She responded, "It's obviously a bad idea. That's how I feel about it!" Next, she was asked, "How do you feel about your relationship with your husband?" Laura responded with a virtual non sequitur: "He's very understanding. He knows what I'm experiencing."

Asked how she felt about any of the significant people or events in her life, Laura couldn't respond. She honestly didn't know how she felt about her husband, her child, her boss, her career, or her life outside her career.

Laura didn't realize that she was responding with opinions, or thoughts, but not feelings. She was so distanced from her own emotions that she needed feedback from a therapist to get on the right track. After several weeks of exercises, Laura learned the difference between thoughts and feelings. Now when she is asked, "How do you feel about your promotion?" she can say, "I hate it!"

As Laura became more aware of her feelings, she found that many of them were negative. Even though it was strange at first, she found that accepting her negative feelings made her feel better about herself. No longer busy fulfilling other people's expectations, Laura could pay attention to her own.

By accepting her own feelings, Laura also learned how to deal with the feelings of those she was responsible for at work. As she began giving effective critiques to the new consultants, Laura found that they welcomed her evaluations, even negative ones, because they were given in clear and constructive terms.

In his book, *Honoring The Self,* psychologist Nathaniel Branden explains that self-confidence is not, as some people mistakenly think, the belief that we will never make an error. Self-confidence is a measure of our ability to cope with life's challenges, not by comparing ourselves with other people's expectations, but using our own standards.

When we don't look for external validation or depend on other people for approval, we can accept disappointment, failure, anger, and criticism, and remain stable in our sense of self. Our sense of identity is not lost in failure, nor is it gained in triumph.

THE SEEDS OF SELF-ESTEEM

In the best of all worlds, we would all be born to perfect parents who give us unconditional love. We would all grow up feeling good about ourselves, and we would develop our highest potential as human beings.

Unconditional Love: Deborah

Deborah grew up in a family that appreciated her for herself. Deborah was a bright girl, and her parents took pleasure in her intellectual development, but they never pressured her to achieve. Deborah's parents shared her successes and defeats, and always let her know that they would support her.

After her first year of college, Deborah wanted to take a year off to travel. Her parents listened to her request, then explained to Deborah that they had set aside enough money to pay for four years of school. The money was for Deborah, and she could use it as she liked. But she also had to deal with the fact that if she spent the money on something other than college, they would not be able to give her more later to finish her degree.

When she understood the financial constraints, Deborah decided to get a job that would pay her to travel. For two years she worked as a researcher for a travel guide company, a job that enabled her to see the world. She also managed to save some money of her own.

When she returned to college, Deborah used her own money and continued working. With the money her parents had saved for her, the family started a travel nest-egg, so they could spend vacations together, visiting places they'd never been.

Deborah is truly fortunate. Her parents accepted her as a person, and respected her individuality. Their love was unconditional, because it was given freely, not reserved until she earned it by pleasing them. Their support was not only financial, but emotional and intellectual. They never tried to buy her love, or tie her down with their expectations.

So when Deborah decided to leave school, she still felt accepted and loved. Even though her parents would not supply unlimited funds, she appreciated their honesty, support, and acceptance.

Having unconditional love from her parents gave Deborah a strong sense of identity. She learned to express her thoughts and feelings openly and to act on her decisions. Instead of seeing her parent's financial restrictions as a disappointment, Deborah considered the situation a challenge. Her belief in herself made it possible to seek the best possible alternative in a complex situation.

THE SEEDS OF SOCIAL ANXIETY

Perhaps because of their own upbringing, many parents equate love with approval. If children perform or behave as expected, then parents respond with love. They believe that this type of conditional behavior is the same as giving positive reinforcement, but it is not. When love is conditional, children must strive for approval. Children know they are not loved for who they *are,* but for what they *do.* Love becomes their reward for performing.

Children who grow up in performance-oriented environments constantly seek approval. Winning acceptance from other people becomes a driving force in their interactions, even with people they love. These children feel a tremendous pressure to achieve, which can continue into their adult life.

Parents seem to have an inexhaustible supply of personalities, qualities, and skills that they expect children to deliver. Some parents desire polite children, others expect a street-smart kid; some expect physical prowess, others scorn athletics; some want a creatively talented child, or a child who can achieve academically; some parents value social graces, while others like children to be seen and not heard.

In some families, the children are never able to match the expectations of the parents. In too many families, the parents have expectations that don't match the realistic capabilities of their children.

Some children are able to compensate by developing a false self, which they present to the world. But the ongoing deceit leaves these children feeling empty or depressed, since their real self is never known or recognized by others. Some children become overly critical of their own performance. Other children withdraw and begin a pattern of avoidance.

Some parents not only withhold love, they are incapable of giving it. Children in these families strive to win approval, always suspecting they won't succeed, but holding on to a tiny seed of hope for the future. These children may grow up to be over-achievers, or they may settle for winning their parents' attention by failing in school, dropping out of teams or organizations, or by becoming delinquents.

Conditional Love: Gretchen

Gretchen was a sensitive child in a family that never spared her feelings. On several occasions, Gretchen's mother reminded her that it was important she learn a trade because she wasn't attractive enough to find a husband.

Gretchen realized that her mother had a point. It was good to learn self-reliance. But her parents could never acknowledge Gretchen's needs. Instead of helping her attend college, they reminded her that she wasn't as smart as her sister, who wanted to be a doctor.

When Gretchen was upset with her parents because they were nicer to her sister, they made fun of her and called her overdramatic.

Gretchen grew up with real problems expressing herself to other people. For many years, she was a recluse. She expressed herself only through her paintings, which she had difficulty showing to others. Perhaps because of the time and effort she put into her work, and perhaps because her work was so personal, Gretchen's paintings were exceptional.

Gretchen's only close friend finally convinced her to take them to a gallery. The gallery owner bought several pieces and arranged for a showing. When he requested that Gretchen be present, she was forced to confront her social withdrawal. Gretchen tried relaxation exercises, started using a journal, and began learning to relate to the world again. By the time her paintings were beginning to sell well, she had learned that her painful feelings were understandable. Acknowledging her childhood deprivation made it possible for Gretchen to respond to those who wanted to know about the source of her artistic inspiration.

Most of us grow up in less-than-perfect environments, with less than one hundred percent of our needs filled by our parents, who also grew up in less-than-perfect situations, trying to fulfill the expectations of their own parents. Very few people survive a childhood of conditional love without some damage to their self-esteem. Other sources of love and acceptance can sometimes compensate for parental deficiencies. Grandparents, teachers, and even babysitters can help by giving love without any preconditions. Friends can help by recognizing the hidden qualities of the child's inner self.

Some children are more sensitive to their upbringing, so their self-esteem will suffer more from negative conditions. Even in the same family, an especially perceptive child will have problems, while a more extroverted child might be less conscious of the lack of parental love or approval. Or, as in Gretchen's family, one child may win parental approval while the other never can.

But people are resilient and can overcome even the most difficult circumstances. It is possible that some children are born with a stronger nervous system and are less damaged by abusive parental influences. Some, like Gretchen, find an outlet for self-expression that allows them to survive and adjust to the deficiencies in their self-esteem, even when other paths of personal communication have been closed.

OUR COMMUNICATION INHERITANCE

Part of accepting ourselves is accepting the less-than-perfect aspects of our personalities. Even more important than knowing how our lack of self-esteem developed is being aware of how it affects our ability to communicate and interact with others. Before we can feel at ease with other people, we must accept who we really are. And before we can do that, we have to *know* who we are.

None of us are born communicators. We learn how to express ourselves from our parents and from our family. We learn the spoken language of our parents, and we also learn from them the subtleties that go beyond words, the nonverbal gestures, inflections, and even the speed of response. We mimic tones and volume, learning to speak loudly or softly in different situations. Each family creates its own code for transmitting emotional meanings.

When parents know themselves and are able to communicate their own feelings, they usually listen and accept the feelings of their children. Early exposure to self-expression helps children to learn to communicate in an authentic and effective way.

When parents are socially anxious, their communications are usually unclear, even with their children. When families hide their feeling behind a stiff upper lip or overexpose them with shouts and curses, children reach adulthood unprepared to express themselves effectively. Then the pattern is repeated into the next generation.

By denying our feelings, we deny who we are. We may share, borrow, or steal the thoughts, ideas, and opinions of others, but our feelings are the fingerprints of our identities. Our emotional response to the world is what makes each of us unique. Unexpressed feelings lead to a lack of self-esteem, which manifests itself as social anxiety.

Communication Inheritance: Anthony

Anthony grew up in a family of six kids, all of whom participated in sports and family activities, but never sat down and shared a conversation. His mother was a meticulous caretaker who made sure her children were well-clothed and well-fed. His father worked hard to support the family. Even though Anthony knew his parents loved him, neither ever told him so in words.

Now that he's an adult, Anthony has problems making decisions. He has little confidence in himself and finds it hard to express his feelings to anyone, including his girlfriend, for whom he cares deeply. He knows she's fed up with his cool veneer, but he can't bring himself to say, "I love you."

Anthony's parents may have been unable to verbalize their emotions. It's possible, even in well-intentioned families, for parents not to reveal feelings, especially when their love seems obvious and is demonstrated by their providing well for their youngsters. Or Anthony's parents simply may have been unaware that *hearing* expressions of love is important to children.

Now Anthony is repeating the pattern. His girlfriend wants spoken commitment of love, but his anxiety prevents him from expressing his feelings. Anthony's potential for happiness depends on his ability to know and express himself.

Communication Inheritance: Kyle

Kyle grew up in a loud, aggressive family. Every meal was like a small war, with Kyle's father and brother arguing and shouting at each other, and Kyle's mother yelling at both of them to shut up. Although his brother still likes to pick fights, Kyle learned early on to avoid them.

In his search for peace and quiet, Kyle now shuns all discussion, whether it's with his wife, a friend, or someone he doesn't know. He's developed a fear that talking will lead to an angry dispute, which he finds intolerable. He spends a great deal of energy trying to please everyone he knows, so they won't get mad and start an argument.

Even though Kyle's family life was very different from Anthony's, he also developed an inability to state his thoughts effectively. The style of communication in Kyle's family inhibited the development of his sense of identity. Kyle managed to survive by avoiding expression, which meant avoiding himself.

Fortunately for those of us who grew up in families with destructive communication patterns, we are all capable of learning healthy new habits of self-expression. Whether we come from families that avoided emotions or from families that exposed feelings inappropriately, we can learn to make our true selves known in a way that increases self-esteem and reduces social anxiety.

WHO YOU ARE WITHOUT SELF-ESTEEM

The mental, emotional, and behavioral patterns that result from low self-esteem can create negative effects on many aspects of your life. The following traits often accompany low self-esteem. As you read through each one, you might find patterns that sound familiar. You might also discover personal characteristics of which you were previously unaware.

The Negative Patterns of Low Self-Esteem

Self-criticism. As you grew up, you took over where your parents and caretakers left off, repeating the negative messages you learned in your childhood. Self-criticism has become an automatic, unrelenting, and unforgiving habit. You may explain to others that you have very high standards, but in truth, your life is a series of compulsory performances. If you execute your routine perfectly, you expect love and acceptance; if not, you feel you deserve ultimate rejection.

Hypersensitivity. You assume that others view you as harshly as you view yourself. You are terribly sensitive to criticism. The slightest hint of a negative remark directed your way feels like a torpedo blast aimed right at your heart.

You are always worried that other people might be scrutinizing you. But because you want their approval, you feel it is necessary to expose at least part of yourself to others. Then, whether it's real or imagined, your fear of their scrutiny paralyzes you.

Insecurity. Whenever you're around other people, you feel vulnerable. Your anxiety arises from a basic lack of confidence in yourself, which leaves you feeling exposed and unprotected. You worry obsessively about what other people will think of your appearance, your intelligence, and your social skills, until you're completely out of touch with reality.

Unrealistic goal-setting. You feel trapped, because there is some higher level you must achieve. Deep inside, you still believe that if you do better than anyone could possibly expect, you will surely win the love and approval you desire. But your efforts rarely pay off, since your goals are unrealistic.

Perfectionism. Striving for excellence is admirable, but there is no such thing as perfection. Yet you feel that a flawless performance is the minimum standard you should achieve. You try to use perfection to win love and acceptance, just as you do when you set unrealistic goals.

John Bradshaw explains in *Healing The Shame That Binds You* that "performance is always related to what is outside the self." As a child, you learn to reach for goals that were not your own. Until you can learn to satisfy yourself, it will be impossible for you to feel a true sense of joy and satisfaction.

Fear of rejection. You always fear that you will not be loved for who you really are. Or, you fear that you have some intrinsic flaw that prevents others from loving you. You fear that if you don't live up to expectations, or if others find out who you really are, they will abandon you.

People-pleasing. Instead of showing your real authentic self, you strive to be conventional and nice. You aim to be what you think others want. When you're successful, you appear socially adept, but every time you achieve this false self, you diminish your sense of identity.

In *Own Your Own Life,* Gary Emery, Ph.D., calls being nice a "social straitjacket." Being nice is often an excuse to avoid your true feelings. When you feel you must always please others, you risk endangering both your mental and physical health.

Avoidance. When you can't manage being nice or fitting yourself into another person's picture of you, you just avoid that person. And when a situation arises that requires you to face people with whom you feel uncomfortable, you find a way to avoid the situation entirely. If you don't put yourself on the line, you don't have to deal with your fear of rejection.

As it is with other forms of pain, avoidance is a natural preventive measure for dealing with anxiety. But over time, you begin to realize that the consequences of avoiding your social anxiety are worse than the benefits.

Self-doubt. You carried the basic sense of uncertainty that all children experience into your adult life. At the most basic level, you doubt yourself. You don't trust your own abilities or your own perceptions. You never really feel sure about how you look, how you dress, or how you articulate. You aren't sure how you feel about others, and you're equally uncertain how you want them to feel about you.

You may have difficulty believing what your eyes and ears tell you. Even your taste buds are suspect. Did the dinner you prepared really taste good, or were your guests just being nice?

Difficulty expressing yourself. How could you tell your parents, whose love you wanted so desperately, that you felt angry or hurt? Now that you're an adult, you worry that any negative feelings or thoughts might alienate others and make them even more inaccessible than they already are. When you do speak, you find it too difficult to disguise your true feelings, so you don't say anything at all.

Difficulty setting boundaries. Because you are unsure of who you are, you internalize whatever other people say about you. Even when someone expresses a negative opinion about you, you accept it. You don't allow yourself to object to any criticism. Making yourself see the world from another person's point of view is necessary for winning their acceptance.

Shame. Because you have given others the power to establish your worth as a human being, you become dependent on other people for approval. When someone doesn't give you whole-hearted love and acceptance, you conclude that some part of yourself must be missing. You can easily develop an extreme case of inadequacy that infects all your relationships.

YOUR COMMUNICATION STYLE

Think about some families you have known and their different styles of communication. How were their verbal and demon-strative styles influenced by their national and ethnic back-grounds, individual temperaments, and family size?

What was your family's style? As a child, were you en-couraged to smile and be quiet no matter what? Or did every-one in your family yell and scream to get attention? How did you fit into your family's communication pattern? Were you the quiet introvert in a boisterous family? Or perhaps the calm-tempered one in a mercurial tribe? Or were you the out-going, adventurous child in a family of ponderous thinkers?

JOURNAL EXERCISE #1

This exercise will help you understand the communication style that you learned from your family. When you write your responses, be as specific as you can.

1. Write a description of your family's communication style. What happened when you wanted to speak up? How did other family members react to you when you did? How did they express themselves?

2. Focus on a specific troublesome incident from your childhood. Perhaps you were punished for something you did or did not do. How did your parents let you know what you did wrong? How did you feel?

3. Now think of an incident that made you feel special. Perhaps you were praised for something you did. What was it? Was it something unusual, or something you were expected to do? How did your parents let you know they were pleased? How did your brothers and sisters react? How did you feel?

If you have difficulty remembering what it was like to be a child in your family, you might try the following exercises. Complete these statements in your journal:

When I was angry, my mother or father would . . .

When I cried, my parents would . . .

If my mother was angry with me, she would . . .

If my father was angry with me, he would . . .

My parents raised their voices when . . .

My parents would hit me when . . .

When you are finished, look for patterns in your responses. Ask yourself what you can learn from these patterns. Just as there are no feelings that are right or wrong, there are no correct or incorrect styles of communication. Good communication simply means that we can express ourselves freely and comfortably. If our communication is based on habit, or if we are inhibited by a lack of communication skills, then we will certainly experience anxiety.

JOURNAL EXERCISE #2

This exercise will help you recognize the source of problems you might have with communication. Once you know your limitations, you can develop tools to overcome them.

1. Describe your current communication style. What patterns have you developed as an adult that are different from those of your family?

2. How well are your current communication patterns working? Do you ever feel that you respond inappropriately? Do you ever wish you could say what you really feel? Do you ever lie about what you really think?

3. Study your answers, and try to determine why you make the choices you do. Do you hope to please someone? Do you want to avoid an argument? Do you feel that it wouldn't be nice to tell the truth?

If you have difficulty starting, try completing these statements in your journal:

When I feel angry with someone, I . . .

When I feel good about someone, I . . .

If someone talks to me in a way I don't like, I . . .

When someone hurts my feelings, I . . .

If someone says something nice to me, I . . .

I ignore people who . . .

People ignore me when . . .

THE HEALING JOURNEY

Although we can't actually travel through time, we can take a healing journey into our past and liberate ourselves from the negative feelings, thoughts, and behaviors we learned as children. By accepting ourselves as we are now, we can change the past that still lives inside us.

When you change your negative patterns, you will experience new emotions. Stretch your awareness, and these new feelings will grow. Soon, you'll become aware that you're developing some positive feelings about yourself.

When you love yourself unconditionally, you accept *all* your thoughts and feelings, even your anxiety. When you can accept yourself as you really are, you can begin to share your feelings with others. Loving and accepting yourself is what makes it possible to actively participate in the world with an inner sense of ease.

JOURNAL EXERCISE #3

This exercise is a healing journey. Instead of feeling trapped by negative habits, begin to develop new ones.

    1. What would it mean to you if you could express yourself freely, clearly, and skillfully? Would your life change in any way? Would any of your relationships be altered?

    2. As you respond to these questions, you might sense a fear or negative thought. If so, write it down.

    3. Now, respond to your negative thought with a realistic appraisal of the situation.

    4. After considering the situation from a new perspective, let yourself express any emotion you feel.

Here's an example:

Sally's Journal

If I could express myself freely, clearly, and skillfully . . .

    Result: People would know what I really think of them. My friends would know when I'm angry with them.

    Fear: I would be exposed. My friends wouldn't like me anymore if they knew how I really felt.

    Realistic response: Why would my friends not like me, just because they know how I really feel? Isn't friendship about accepting and loving each other through thick and thin? Besides, I'm sure I show my anger in other ways, by acting childish or resentful.

    If I could express my anger skillfully, my friends wouldn't have to guess what I'm thinking, and we could solve our problems better. If someone decides not to be friends with me because I'm honest, then that's their decision. I'm not responsible for anyone else's actions. That person wouldn't be such a great friend, anyway.

    Reaction: By expressing myself, I can have honest communications with people I care about. Maybe my friends will be more open with me, too. That's an intriguing idea, learning how my friends *really* feel. I feel exhilarated!

4 EXPRESS YOURSELF WITH EASE

Although [you] have fight and flight in common with the lower animals . . . you are not instinctively forced to do either. Instead, you have the human option to talk with others and in that way to cope with what is bothering you.

DR. MANUEL SMITH
When I Say No, I Feel Guilty

Maybe you want to give voice to your ideas and feelings, but whenever you try, you feel out of control. It may seem that you have only two choices: either keep your feelings to yourself, or risk being overwhelmed. If expressing yourself to other people is something you avoid at any cost, then you're experiencing another of the painful consequences of social anxiety.

Because many of us were brought up to disregard or devalue our own feelings and thoughts, the idea of opening up to others can seem overwhelming. But no matter how difficult it seems, we are all capable of expressing our inner selves. By expressing ourselves, we are able to share our life with others.

In his book on assertiveness training, *When I Say No, I Feel Guilty*, Manuel Smith, Ph.D., points out that the ability to communicate with words is what distinguishes humans from all other forms of life. Only humans can solve their problems by talking them out.

When you started reading this book, you recognized a problem: you wanted to feel more comfortable around people. Each time you work with your journal, you're making an effort to solve your problem by getting in touch with your feelings. The next step is to learn how to express your feelings out loud without being overwhelmed by anxiety.

THE HIGH COST OF HIDING

When you express your true self to others, you put yourself in a position of risk. Other people might *not* like what you think. They might criticize you for feeling the way you do. They might reject you for your beliefs. In fact, you are almost guaranteed that some will.

But think of the alternatives. If you don't express yourself, others will have to make assumptions. If you won't show your true self, others will have to guess what's going on inside you. They might guess what you want them to guess, or they might not. Either way, you're letting someone else decide who you are.

Hiding our genuine selves from others is giving away control and giving away control is giving away self-respect. When we express ourselves, we are telling other people that we know and accept ourselves. We take control of who we are by letting other people know what we think, feel, and believe.

Remaining silent isn't the only way we give away control. We also avoid self-expression when we fake agreement—rationalizing that we're polite. Or, in a moment of pain, we may hurl our anger at others—another ineffective means of communicating. If we don't take time to analyze our emotions, we can't express ourselves appropriately.

Self-expression is a way to take responsibility for ourselves and to draw boundaries between ourselves and others.

When we express who we are, we increase our sense of self-worth by giving away the desire to control someone else's actions and reactions. Instead of hoping for other people's approval, we are approving of ourselves.

If the idea of speaking out seems impossible to you, remember that you constantly express yourself in other ways. Your facial expressions, your tone of voice, your posture, your body language, all send messages to other people about your inner self. If you are sending these nonverbal messages out to the world anyway, why not learn to speak clearly and effectively, using self-assertive communication?

WHAT IS SELF-ASSERTIVE COMMUNICATION?

Self-assertive communication is the expression of our most authentic selves. In *Honoring The Self,* psychologist Nathaniel Branden says that "Every act of self-assertion is an implicit affirmation of [our] right to exist." When we assert ourselves, we assert our value.

Self- Assertive Communication: Betty

Betty is a housewife who has supported her husband's career, and seen their three daughters through school. Now that the girls are on their own, Betty has some spare time, and she's taken up painting. When her husband, Paul, first noticed Betty with her artist's supplies, he laughed.

Betty's response was to hide her work from her husband. She told herself that his reaction didn't matter. But it did. Every time she thought about painting, she felt anxious and irritable, and remaining silent made her feel worse.

At first Betty ruminated about the incident, playing it over and over in her mind, wondering what she should have said when he laughed. Then she realized that by actually writing down what she was thinking and feeling, she could focus more specifically on the source of her unease. She was able to look beyond her feelings of anxiety about her husband's reaction and see the distorted thought patterns that were creating her painful feelings about herself.

Distorted thought patterns act like unconscious road blocks. Instead of getting a clear message about our inner selves so we can express it to others, we get negative readings that send us down unproductive side streets. When we recognize a distorted thought for what it is, we can remove the road block and continue down the main road toward effective self-expression.

BETTY'S JOURNAL

What happened: Paul criticized my painting, and I didn't say anything.

I feel: Terrible.

My thoughts: Nothing I do counts for anything. Why bother? Unless I'm helping somebody else, nothing I do matters.

Distorted thought patterns: I'm generalizing!—Why do I say "nothing" and "anything?"
My thinking is win or lose—I don't feel great about what happened, so I feel terrible. Since Paul doesn't approve of my painting, it doesn't count.

Are these thoughts true? No! Certainly many of the things I've done in my life have counted, and been appreciated. It doesn't matter what Paul thinks, because my painting counts to me. It makes me feel good, and that's what matters.

New thought: Just because Paul laughed at my painting doesn't make it nothing. Or me nothing. I've probably laughed at him before, without knowing how it felt.

How else could I express myself? Just tell Paul how I really feel.

The next step was difficult for Betty. Although she was able to imagine an action that would help her feel better, and she wanted to tell Paul how she felt, she still believed that talking about her pain would make her feel worse. What if Paul didn't understand? What if they ended up in an argument? Analyzing her thoughts helped to relieve some of Betty's anxiety, but she still felt frustrated. As a final effort, she decided to attempt self-assertion.

> The next time Paul saw Betty painting, he made a little joke about living with Picasso. Instead of reacting to Paul's comment, Betty thought about how *she* felt about her work. She said to Paul, "My painting means a lot to me. I feel hurt when you make fun of it."
>
> Paul's face dropped. It was clear that he had not intended to hurt his wife. "I'm sorry," he told her. "I really think it's great that you've got this new interest. I guess I'm a little scared. If you get so involved with your painting, you won't be spending all your time with me."

Betty's ability to express what she was feeling made it possible for her to deal with a negative situation, and to turn it into a positive one. She learned what her husband's real feelings were, and she told him how important it was to her that he express himself clearly.

What made it possible for Betty to speak up was that she had examined her own reactions carefully and accepted them. Having recognized her feelings as valid, Betty was able to expose the distorted thinking that underlay her hurt. From there, she could move on to more realistic thoughts, which allowed her to feel positive about herself.

When Betty expressed how important her painting was to her, she was *owning* her thoughts. When she told her husband that she felt hurt, she was owning her feelings. She did not displace the responsibility for her feelings onto Paul by saying, "You made me feel bad." Instead of seeing herself as a victim, Betty took control by owning her inner self.

When you know what you think and feel, the idea of sharing your inner self with others will feel less overwhelming. When you are clear with yourself, you can be clear to others. Rather than losing your self, you will begin to feel stronger about yourself. Assertion is a refreshing change from the pervasive anxiety you feel when you repress your authentic self.

Assertion versus Aggression

Some people reserve self-assertion for a power play, a tactic to save face when they've been emotionally trampled. Other people view their communications as sophisticated games; if they play just right, they'll come out on top.

Self-assertion is neither a tactic nor a game. Self-assertion is simply an expression of your inner reality. The power of self-assertion is its utter simplicity and absolute honesty. Self-assertion does not require any special skill or talent. When you know yourself, accept yourself, and express yourself, you gain power over yourself, not over others.

Self-assertive communication won't get you anything but self-respect. Self-assertion is not something you can use to bully other people, but it is a tool you can use when people try to bully you.

But What About Being Nice?

In *Healing The Shame That Binds You,* John Bradshaw points out that being nice is "primarily a way of manipulating people and situations." By being nice, you avoid conflict, but you also avoid intimacy. When you catch yourself being nice, ask yourself if you are really being honest. Perhaps what you are doing is trying to please others just to win their approval.

Do I Have To Tell Everything?

Self-assertive communication involves making choices. Each of us is responsible for our own inner world. Each act of self-expression involves a choice about which aspects of our thoughts, emotions, and beliefs are appropriate to the situation and which would lead to effective communication.

Self-Assertive Communication: Sam

Sam had just started working for a law firm, when he was invited to a party given by a coworker he knew only slightly. Sam and his wife, Patty, were talking with a small group when one of the men encouraged another to repeat a joke for Sam's benefit. Sam didn't realize until the punchline that the joke was mildly racist. He smiled uncomfortably and exchanged glances with Patty, who also looked uncomfortable.

When the man started another joke more blatantly racist than the first Patty elbowed Sam and headed for the kitchen. When the man finished the joke, Sam smiled meekly and went to look for his wife. In the kitchen, Patty asked Sam why he hadn't said anything. He asked why *she* hadn't. "They're your friends," Patty argued. "They're not my friends," Sam told her. "They're people from work. I barely know them. What am I supposed to do, tell them their jokes stink and so do they?"

Sam and Patty were in a difficult situation, which was compounded by the fact that both of them were new to the group. Sam sensed that his anger was not an appropriate response, especially with people he scarcely knew. But he didn't feel comfortable asserting himself, because he was the newest member of their firm and would be working with them every day. But instead of acknowledging his own feelings of discomfort, Sam displaced his emotions to his coworkers, and concluded that working with racists was the cause of his anxiety.

Sam and Patty left the party a few minutes later, both feeling anxious. Sam was uncomfortable leaving early, but he knew that Patty didn't want to stay. Patty felt guilty for making Sam leave before he was ready, but after the incident, she really didn't want to spend more time at the party.

Sam felt disappointed with himself for not speaking out about the jokes. He didn't know what he could have said to make the evening turn out better, but he wished he'd said something.

Sam acted responsibly by not reacting with anger to the offensive jokes, but there were other ways he could have asserted himself that would have been both appropriate and effective. The most obvious action Sam could have taken was acknowledging his own feelings of discomfort when the man began telling the second joke.

Sam could have said exactly what he was feeling, "Oh, no. Not another racist joke." Or he could have explained his wife's sudden departure by saying, "Excuse me, but my wife and I feel uneasy with that type of joke." Or he could have gone to the kitchen with his wife and not stayed to listen to the second unpleasant joke.

Any of the three responses would have maintained Sam's self-esteem, because in all three he would have acknowledged and expressed his feelings of discomfort. With our self-expression, we claim our right to exist. The mere act of acknowledging ourselves brings a feeling of power. Any self-expression makes us feel better, whether or not it has an effect on the cause of our discomfort.

Sam and his wife took their unpleasant experience seriously, and made efforts to learn how to deal with such situations. Here are some pages from Sam's and Patty's journal exercises.

SAM'S JOURNAL

What happened: I didn't like that guy telling racist jokes, but I didn't say anything.

I feel: Impotent, frustrated, hypocritical.

My thoughts: I'm as much of a jerk as the guy telling the joke. I should have said something. I disappointed Patty and ruined the evening. If that's what the people in my new office are like, I may as well give up on trying to make new friends.

Distorted thought patterns: I'm generalizing—making global conclusions—and predicting the future." I'm assuming that all the people in the office are like the guy who told jokes I didn't appreciate, and that I'll never make any friends.

Is it true? I don't know that my predictions are true. Just because one guy's a jerk, doesn't mean the others are like that at all. For all I know, some of them might respect me for speaking out.

More distorted though patterns: Generalizing again—I called myself a jerk, just because I didn't deal with the situation very well. I don't deserve that label.

You must/you should—I give myself a hard time because I wish I had said something, but I didn't know what to say! It was a difficult situation to deal with.

Win-or-lose thinking—I'm blaming myself for ruining the evening, and I didn't even do anything! Why did I let that incident ruin my night?

New thought: That was really an uncomfortable situation, and I really didn't handle it as well as I'd have liked. But that doesn't make me a jerk, or impotent, and it doesn't mean that I have to go out and find a new job, or that Patty won't respect me. It was difficult for her, too, or she would have said something herself.

Next time? One thing's for sure, I won't stand there and listen to a joke like that. If I'd just walked away, I would have felt better. And maybe I'll be able to say something next time. At least I'll be able to admit to Patty that something like that makes me feel bad, too.

PATTY'S JOURNAL

What happened: Sam and I got into an argument because that guy was telling racist jokes at the party, and neither of us said anything.

I feel: Guilty, dirty.

My thoughts: Sam's new office must be full of creeps. Practically the first people we talk to, and they tell racist jokes. Sam must feel insecure because he didn't even say anything. I guess this means I won't be spending much time with him when he's around these people. What a rotten evening.

Distorted thought patterns: I'm generalizing—making global conclusions. From one creepy guy, or two, I imagine an office of creeps.

I'm mind reading—I assume that his not saying anything means that Sam is insecure. What about me? I didn't say anything, either!

I'm predicting the future—already envisioning years of frustration for myself and Sam, just because of one unpleasant incident.

True thoughts?   No, my thoughts aren't true, they're really distorted. I didn't even meet most of the people at the party. I don't have any idea what the other people Sam works with are like. Sam might feel insecure, but I don't know that.

New thoughts?   It looks like I'm putting my own feelings about the situation onto Sam. If I assume things are going to work out badly, then I'm not really giving it a chance. One bad night at one party really isn't a reason to write off Sam's new job.

Next time?   Instead of assuming that Sam should deal with it, I'll try to just say what I think and feel. If I had just said, "Sam, I don't want to hear this, I'll see you later," I would have been able to move on and meet some other people, and the whole incident would have been really insignificant.

Sam and Patty learned a great deal about themselves from their negative experience. Chances are that next time they find themselves in an uncomfortable situation, they'll be better equipped to express themselves appropriately and effectively.

Sam and Patty both realized that when they were willing to look at their inner selves and take responsibility for their feelings, they gained self-respect, and their symptoms of anxiety decreased.

Assertiveness enhances self-esteem.

JOURNAL EXERCISE #1

This exercise will help you uncover distorted thought patterns that might be influencing you. As you complete each step, writing down your thoughts and feelings, you will begin to find more realistic ways of thinking about yourself and your experiences.

1. When you find yourself feeling the need to express something, or wishing you were able to say something, stop and write down exactly what happened, and what you are feeling.
2. Now, write down any thoughts that come to you about the situation, about yourself, or about the person with whom you were talking.
3. Were any of your thoughts examples of distorted thinking? (You might want to go back and review chapter 2. Which distortions are shaping your thoughts? List them.
4. Using what you've learned about distorted thinking, ask yourself if your thoughts were really true. If they weren't, do you now have a more realistic understanding about the situation you experienced? Write down any new thoughts and feelings that come to you.
5. You should now see a new way of thinking, based on a realistic evaluation of yourself and the situation you experienced. Based on your new realistic thoughts, try to imagine some responses you might make next time, responses that would express your real feelings effectively.

What If I Don't Know How I Feel?
Sometimes it's difficult to identify our feelings and formulate an assertive expression, especially when someone throws a comment at you that is particularly upsetting. Then you relive

the experience later, wishing you had come back with the perfect response.

If not knowing the right thing to say is a frustrating experience for you, it doesn't have to be. You may not be equipped to be a television talk show host, able to deliver clever repartee at the drop of a hat. But when you know your own mind, you can handle any situation.

A simple, uncomplicated statement of who you are and what you're feeling at the moment is always a good response. Even if you say, "I'm not sure how I feel about that," you're making an assertive statement that is an honest reflection of your inner self.

Whenever you find yourself at a loss for a response, pause for a moment and reflect on your freedom of choice. You don't have to answer in a certain way, just because the person asking the question seems to want you to. Try to be aware of your feelings so you can maintain your self-respect.

Self-Assertive Communication: Marsha
Marsha grew up in a controlled, unemotional family. Feelings were never discussed; the children were told to keep a "stiff upper lip." Marsha went to law school and became one of the top litigators in her firm, excelling at courtroom persuasion. But in other facets of her life, Marsha's communications were breaking down.

In the office, Marsha had difficulty getting the secretarial staff to complete her work on time. She felt irritated during her performance review with the firm's senior partner. At home, Marsha realized she didn't like the way her husband was dealing with the family budget, but she felt paralyzed at the idea of confronting him. And she even found it difficult to tell her nine-year-old daughter how impressed she was with the work the child was doing in school.

Marsha tried to ease her sense of anxiety by telling herself that she was an intellectual, that emotionality was not her style. She was aware of her anxiety, and she identified this as her problem. She didn't realize that anxiety was only the symptom of her real problem: her inability to recognize and accept her own feelings.

When her anxiety began to be noticed by other attorneys, Marsha realized that she needed to pay closer attention to her problem, before it became a critical impediment at work. She read everything she could find about anxiety, and she discovered that anxiety was a symptom of her inability to be authentic.

Over the next few months, Marsha worked on exercises that helped her get in touch with her feelings. Then she started learning how to express them, using self-assertive communication. She was nervous at first because not many people she knew spoke frankly about themselves. But she realized that the more she voiced her feelings, the less anxiety she felt.

Marsha even learned to admit to an occasional sense of inadequacy, and when she did, she found that people responded positively. To her surprise, her clients seemed to be much more trusting when she was open with them about her feelings. Instead of seeing herself as the aggressive attorney, Marsha learned to think of herself as an effective communicator. She even discovered that she got as much pleasure sharing confidences with her daughter as she did from winning trials.

THE FEELING VOCABULARY

Feelings are the primary language of self-assertion. Experiencing the true freedom of self-expression means moving beyond the arena of thoughts and opinions. Even though we acknowledge our emotional state by expressing how we feel in the moment, we can still allow ourselves to be flexible, so our feelings can change freely, in response to outside events.

Look at the Feeling Vocabulary. Do you recognize any of your own emotions in the list? Can you add any feelings to the Vocabulary?

FEELING VOCABULARY

POSITIVE			
INTENSE	**STRONG**	**MODERATE**	**MILD**
loved adored idolized	enchanted ardor infatuated tender	liked cared-for esteemed affectionate fond	friendly regarded benevolent
alive	vibrant independent capable happy great proud gratified	excited patient strong gay good inspired anticipating strong amused	wide-awake at ease relaxed comfortable content keen amazed alert sensitive
wanted lustful worthy pity respected empathy awed	worthy passionate admired sympathetic important concerned appreciated consoled	secure yearning popular peaceful appealing determined	sure attractive approved untroubled graceful
elated enthusiastic zealous	delighted eager optimistic joyful courageous hopeful	pleased excited interested jolly relieved glad	turned-on warm amused
courageous	valiant brave brilliant	venturous peaceful intelligent	daring comfortable smart

FEELING VOCABULARY

NEGATIVE			
MILD	MODERATE	STRONG	INTENSE
unpopular	suspicious	disgusted	hated
	envious	resentful	unloved
	enmity	bitter	abhorred
	aversion	detested	loathed
		fed-up	despised
listless	dejected	frustrated	angry
moody	unhappy	sad	hurt
lethargic	bored	depressed	miserable
gloomy	bad	sick	pain
dismal	forlorn	disconsolate	lonely
discontented	disappointed	dissatisfied	cynical
tired	wearied	fatigued	exhausted
indifferent	torn-up	worn-out	worthless
unsure	inadequate	useless	impotent
impatient	ineffectual	weak	futile
dependent	helpless	hopeless	abandoned
unimportant	resigned	forlorn	estranged
regretful	apathetic	rejected	degraded
	shamed	guilty	
bashful	shy	embarrassed	humiliated
self-conscious	uncomfortable	inhibited	alienated
puzzled	baffled	bewildered	shocked
edgy	confused	frightened	panicky
upset	nervous	anxious	trapped
reluctant	tempted	dismayed	horrified
timid	tense	apprehensive	afraid
mixed-up	worried	dreadful	scared
	perplexed	disturbed	terrified
	troubled		threatened
sullen	disdainful	antagonistic	infuriated
provoked	contemptuous	vengeful	furious
	alarmed		

JOURNAL EXERCISE #2

This exercise will help you become more aware of the many diverse feelings you experience every day. Your goal is to gain a constant awareness of your emotional state.

1. Keep a list of the feelings you experience during an entire day. Try to write down each emotion as you become aware of it. Use the Feeling Vocabulary list to help you find the word or words that best describes it.

2. At regular intervals during the day, after each meal, for example, stop whatever you're doing and read over your list. If you become aware of some feelings that you have omitted, add them to the list.

3. Repeat the exercise each day for at least a week. You'll probably be surprised by the number and variety of moods and feelings that you've listed.

THE LANGUAGE OF SELF-ASSERTION

Self-assertive expression allows us to express our inner selves to the people in our world. But it also allows us to draw boundaries between other people's thoughts and feelings and our own. When we know how we feel, we can deal with other people's feelings without assuming guilt or assigning blame.

Reflective Speaking

Reflective speaking is a method for developing self-assertive communications. By answering someone with their own words, you *reflect* what is said to you, and prevent yourself from assuming responsibility for the feelings expressed by the other person.

When Marsha was learning to work on her self-expressive communications, she realized that part of her anxiety came from accepting whatever was said to her as true. When the senior partner in her firm told her, "I really don't like the way you've prepared this report," Marsha felt incompetent.

Knowing that it was important to stay in touch with her feelings, Marsha went back into her office and added these feelings to her vocabulary: ineffectual, impatient, regretful.

Being able to recognize and accept her feelings was a big change for Marsha. But she also had to learn to separate her true feelings from the emotions she assumed she should have. In her journal, Marsha practiced making an assertive response using the reflective speaking technique.

MARSHA'S JOURNAL

When my boss said: I don't like the way you've prepared this report.

I took his words as a criticism of myself. I accepted his words as implying a negative "truth" about me.

I could have said: You think I shouldn't have done the report this way? or, You think the report should be done a different way?

By constructing a reflective answer to her boss, repeating his own words, Marsha realized that his opinion of the report was just that: a comment on a particular assignment, not an indictment of Marsha as a person. By responding with a reflective statement, Marsha could open up communications with her boss and give herself an opportunity to learn from him.

Working on the reflective speaking exercise demonstrated to Marsha the negative effect her behavior had created. Obviously, Marsha had done her best in making the report, but instead of reminding herself of that, she had been ready to assume the responsibility for her boss's opinion. Blaming herself was a self-defeating reaction that only stirred more negative feelings about herself.

The next day, Marsha asked her secretary, Mrs. Lindbloom, to make some changes in the report, print it, and give a copy to the senior partner. Mrs. Lindbloom shrugged, and said, "If that's really how you want me to do it."

Marsha felt the usual tightening feeling in her stomach and throat, but she took a deep breath, and tried to discern what she was feeling. She identified a sense of loss and confusion. She took another deep breath and said, "I'm confused. You asked if this is really how I want you to do it. Do you think I should do it differently?"

Marsha prepared herself, expecting Mrs. Lindbloom to turn away or give an angry response. Instead, Mrs. Lindbloom opened the report and pointed to the pages that were to be changed. She explained that when the other lawyers made changes for the senior partner, they showed him the changes separately. Only after he approved them was the entire report reprinted.

Marsha's efforts to communicate resulted in several positive changes. Instead of feeling bad about herself after confrontations with her boss and secretary, she was able to recognize these positive emotions and add them to her list: hopeful, approved, amazed.

Marsha made a separate note in her journal to remind herself that admitting her confusion to Mrs. Lindbloom had resulted in their first positive interaction in several weeks. By not assuming that Mrs. Lindbloom's remark was meant as a personal "jab," Marsha had been able to learn something new about office procedure.

Reflective statements may sound a bit artificial when you first begin using them, but they can still be effective. In addition to the mirroring action these statements have on the other person, they allow you time to reflect on your own thoughts and feelings. Reflective speaking can be a useful tool while you're learning assertive communication.

JOURNAL EXERCISE #3

Every minute of every day, you create your own reality. This exercise will help you become more aware of the decisions you make on a minute-to-minute basis. Being conscious of your freedom to choose makes it easier for you to take responsibility for yourself.

1. For one entire day, try to be conscious of every thought, feeling, perception, and intuition you have, and every action you make.

2. Keep a running mental commentary on each moment. You might describe your day like this:

I'm choosing to get out of bed now.

I'm now choosing to brush my teeth.

I'm now choosing to walk over to the closet.

I'm now choosing the clothes I want to wear.

Now, I decide to open the curtain.

Now, I'm going to look out the window.

3. Make notes in your journal at least three times each day. How are you doing with this exercise? Are you finding it difficult to be aware of yourself?

4. Did you discover any times during your day that you gave away your freedom of choice to others? Were there times when you did what someone else wanted?

5. Were there times when your thoughts were not truly your own?

6. Repeat the entire exercise at least one more day.

Interpretation

Interpretation is a second technique you can practice for becoming an assertive communicator. When you *interpret* what another person says to you, you assert your freedom to see the situation differently. You clearly separate yourself from responsibility for what was said. By asking what was meant and what the feeling behind the statement was, you establish that the other person "owns" the statement, not you.

Self-Assertive Communication: Bob

Bob teaches at a large university in the Southeast. He and his wife were divorced several years ago, when Bob was thirty-seven. So far none of his dates have led to long-

term relationships, but Bob still hopes to find a permanent relationship.

Bob's friend from work, Marty, is happily married.
Whenever Marty and his wife meet a likely prospect for
Bob, they try to arrange a date. Bob feels a lot of pressure
from Marty. Not just about who to go with, but about
dating in general, and about his ability to relate to
women. Bob feels very anxious whenever they talk about
women, but it seems to be Marty's favorite topic.

When Bob invited a woman professor they both
knew to go out to dinner with him, Marty couldn't help
commenting on Bob's choice. "I don't think you should
go out with her," he told Bob. "She's too tall for you."

Using the techniques for assertive self-expression, Bob had
several choices of response. First, he answered reflectively.

Marty: I don't think you should go out with her, Bob,
she's much too tall for you.
Bob: You think that since she's taller than I am, I shouldn't
go out with her.

Bob's statement reflected Marty's words back to him. His response did not take responsibility for Marty's thought, but it
did allow Bob time to consider his own thoughts and feelings.

Bob had no problem going out with a woman who was
taller than himself, but it seemed that Marty thought this was a
problem. Bob tried to find out, by interpreting Marty's
comments.

Marty: Yeah. There's plenty of women around, Bob.
Why make yourself uncomfortable?
Bob: It sounds like you feel uncomfortable with me
going out with someone who's taller than I am.

By interpreting Marty's words, Bob was able to keep his own
feelings and thoughts separate from Marty's. The interpreta-

tive statement also let Bob try to clarify the meaning of what Marty said.

> Marty: You mean you don't feel uncomfortable? She's at least six inches taller than you are, Bob.
> Bob: No. It doesn't bother me at all. I like her, Marty. She's easy to talk to. We have a lot in common. She's also very attractive.
> Marty: Sure she is, but *tall*.
> Bob: Yeah. I think tall women are really attractive.
> Marty: And she said she'd go out with you?
> Bob: Friday night!

What surprised Bob the most about his use of self-assertive communication was that he found himself enjoying his ability to say what he really felt. He no longer felt pressured. By accepting Marty's opinions instead of voicing his own, Bob had been giving away control of his life. His feelings of pressure were his own reaction to his inability to express himself.

The I Statement
The first two methods of self-assertive communication separate you from the thoughts and feelings expressed by other people when they speak to you. A third technique of self-assertive communication will help you open the door to your inner self, so you can express who you really are.

This method is called the *I statement* because it uses the first person voice to remind you as you speak that you are responsible for what is being said. Your goal is to express your feelings, thoughts, and beliefs, always beginning each statement with the first person pronoun. The I statement will help you focus on your inner truth.

Self-Assertive Communication: Marianne
Marianne is very active in her community's environmental action group. Even though she's been asked often, she refuses to accept a leadership position because speaking

in front of others makes her anxious. Nonetheless, she's always available to help with the group's efforts.

Recently, the chairman of the group asked Marianne to lead the waste management committee. "The committee needs guidance, Marianne. We really need someone like you to take an active role."

Marianne's first thought was to say, "Please don't ask me to take on that responsibility. Speaking in front of a group makes me too nervous."

Before she actually said anything out loud, Marianne realized that her answer was not an I statement; it was also not a true representation of her feelings. Being forced to respond to the chairman increased Marianne's feelings of discomfort.

She took a deep breath and concentrated for a moment on her own feelings. She really didn't want to lead the committee, but that didn't make her an inadequate person. One of the reasons Marianne got involved with the group in the first place was her strong commitment to being a helping person.

Instead of answering, Marianne told the chairman that she would think about the offer overnight. At home, she worked on various ways to express her real feelings.

MARIANNE'S JOURNAL

When the chairman said: "We really need someone like you to take an active role,"

I could have said: "You think the committee needs someone who can take an active role," (reflective statement)

Or, I could have said: "You think I'm someone who can take an active role," or, "It sounds like you think taking an active role is the same as taking a leadership role" (interpretative statement).

Marianne realized that for a moment she had accepted the chairman's statement, that the committee needed her as a leader because she was an active member of the group. Accepting this opinion as true gave Marianne feelings of inadequacy and shame. If the chairman was right, then something must be wrong with Marianne, because she did not feel comfortable with the leadership position.

Answering the chairman reflectively might have given Marianne the time she needed to remember her own feelings about this sensitive issue and separate herself from the chairman's opinion of her. Going further and interpreting the chairman's words could have helped her clarify their differences of opinion.

By taking the exercises home and working on them, Marianne realized that her feelings about herself were quite different from the chairman's opinion of her. When she didn't feel pressured, Marianne was able to come up with a response that expressed her true feelings and allowed her to be in control of her decision.

> The next day, Marianne called the chairman and said, "Thank you for offering me the position. I'm glad that you recognized that I want to take an active role, but I'm not yet ready to take a leadership role."

In addition to helping us focus, I statements help us to avoid blaming. When we blame other people or difficult situations for our feelings, we're allowing something outside ourselves to orchestrate our feelings. In blaming, we give up control of our lives.

RESPONSIBILITY LEADS TO FREEDOM

Accepting responsibility for the feelings we want to express is a major step toward decreasing the anxiety in our lives. I statements show that we have a definite relationship with our world. Even if the feelings we choose to reveal aren't those we wish we had , I statements show that we are in control, that we know ourselves, and that we can accept ourselves as less than perfect.

Self-Assertive Communication: Dana

Dana is dealing with dating, something she's avoided because her husband died a year ago. Dana still feels like everything in her life is beyond her control. When a friend tried to get Dana to go on a double date, Dana refused. She told her friend, "Being on a date just makes me feel too upset."

Dana's statement, while an effort to be honest, really didn't reflect what she was experiencing. Instead, it increased her sense of being out of control. Dana spent some time learning to be more self-assertive. She learned to focus on herself, not on other people or situations.

After completing several exercises, Dana was able to explain herself this way: "I don't want to go out with anyone right now. I'm still having a difficult time. I'm not ready to start dating." This assertive I statement made Dana's feelings known, and at the same time, it allowed her to gain some control of her life, by claiming her freedom to make choices.

Self-Assertive Communication: Richard

Richard works as a department manager in a large retail company. He's unhappy with his position. He wants to move up, but the store manager has told him that the company needs him to stay where he is. Richard has put off looking elsewhere, because, as he says, "Interviewers drive me crazy."

Richard's statement revealed his anxiety, but it put all control for his thoughts and feelings into the hands of the interviewers. Before Richard could deal with any job search, he needed to put his feelings about himself into focus.

Richard completed several exercises and was able to connect with his thoughts and feelings, which helped him understand his anxiety about interviews. He discovered that he was displacing his own negative beliefs about himself onto the interview, assuming that any potential interviewer would see him as a loser.

Richard also realized that he considered his work the most important aspect of his life, and his new job as crucial for his future. Elevating his work above every other part of his life increased the pressure Richard felt in his present job, along with the anxiety he felt when he thought about looking for a new one.

Richard also found out that he was generalizing, by labeling himself and identifying himself with his job. Because his manager refused to promote him, Richard assumed he was worthless. Because he felt apprehensive about looking for a new job, Richard considered himself a hopeless failure, destined to stay in unhappy circumstances forever.

By identifying so closely with his work, Richard put up a mental roadblock, preventing himself from dealing effectively with disappointments in his present position, which then made it difficult for him to think constructively about future possibilities. The only way to escape from his dead end was for Richard to learn to separate himself from his job.

His new awareness didn't remove all his anxiety overnight, but he did learn a new focus for dealing with interviews.

> Richard applied for a job at a company with strong growth potential. In the middle of the interview, he began to sweat profusely, and then his heart started beating quickly. Before he lost control, Richard said to the man interviewing him, "I'm feeling somewhat nervous, because this job is really important to me."

Richard found that expressing himself so openly made him feel much more comfortable. Instead of worrying about his anxiety, he could concentrate on the subject at hand. He was called back for a second interview, so admitting his feelings seemed to be a positive move.

JOURNAL EXERCISE #4

Becoming more adept at self-assertive communication takes practice. Use your journal to experiment with different ways to respond to negative, irritating, or confrontational statements.

1. For one week, collect any statements people make to you that set off your symptoms of anxiety and write them in your journal.
2. Make a brief note after each statement, reminding yourself what you felt in response. If you answered the person, write down what you actually said.
3. After each statement, write down different ways you *might* have responded. Write at least one reflective response, one interpretative response, and one I statement.

Here are some examples from the journals of Betty, Marsha, Richard, and Dana.

BETTY'S JOURNAL

Yesterday, my sister Ida and I were having lunch, when Ida said, "You always make me feel self-conscious."

I said nothing. I ignored it. Then I felt bad later and wished I'd answered her. What could I have said? How could I have asserted myself?

I could have used a reflective answer: "You feel self-conscious around me, Ida?"

Or an interpretative response: "Do you feel like I'm trying to upset you, Ida?"

Or an I statement: "I'm sorry that you feel uncomfortable, Ida. I'd like to know what's upset you."

MARSHA'S JOURNAL

My colleague, Andy, was behind me in the cafeteria today. When I picked up my tray, he looked at me and said, "I've always liked you, Marsh, but sometimes you drive me crazy."

I didn't say anything, just smiled. But the comment really irritated me. I really wanted to know what he was talking about. What other ways could I have answered?

> *Reflective*
> *response:* "You feel like you're crazy when you're around me?"
>
> *Interpretative:* "Are you saying you feel irritated when you're around me?"
>
> *I statement:* "I'm glad to know you like me, Andy, but I'm not sure what you mean when you say crazy."

RICHARD'S JOURNAL

I had my job interview today with the regional manager of the company I'd like to work for. It seemed like the interview went well, but then I asked her when she'd be making her decision. She looked uncomfortable and said, "You really put me on the spot."

I said, "Oh, sorry."

Then she smiled and went on to small talk. I never found out when she'd be making her decision, or why she didn't want to tell me. I wish I'd answered more assertively. I could have said:

> *Reflective*
> *response:* "You feel like you're on the spot?"
>
> *Interpretative:* "Are you saying that my question is in some way inappropriate?"

I statement: "I'm sorry you feel uncomfortable with my question. I didn't intend to push you, I'm just eager to know your decision."

DANA'S JOURNAL

After business school this evening, some of the class wanted to go to a bar, but I didn't want to join them. One of the men I don't know very well said, "You sure know how to spoil a good time." I didn't know how to answer him. I could have answered:

Reflective response: "You were having a good time, and I did something to change that?"

Interpretative response: "Do you think you can't have a good time unless I go with you?"

I statement: "I'm sorry you feel that way. I'm surprised that your good time depends on me."

PRACTICE MAKES IT WORK

Dana noticed that writing about the incident in her journal relieved much of the anxiety she felt the next time she attended her evening class. At first, it took some time for her to come up with appropriate, self-assertive answers, even on paper. But as she practiced, she began to get better, and within a few weeks, she was able to practice out loud.

Using self-assertive statements may feel unnatural at first. The structure of a reflective or interpretative response can seem awkward, but practicing these statements will make them more comfortable. It may take a little more time and practice to feel natural asserting yourself with I statements, especially if you're not used to speaking out. But even during the practice stages, you'll usually get positive reactions that will encourage your efforts.

Making self-assertive statements taught Dana something about herself and about other people. Before doing her exercise, she'd assumed that the irritating man in her class was purposely insulting her. After reviewing her journal exercise, Dana realized that the man might have been awkwardly trying to say something nice.

When we can see that an obnoxious remark might actually be an awkward compliment, we're on the road to understanding social anxiety. None of us are perfect, and when we learn to accept our own defects, we can also accept flaws in others. When we understand and accept ourselves, we are better able to appreciate others, and the world begins to feel like a more welcoming place.

5 AT EASE WITH YOURSELF

We live in an atmosphere of shame. We are ashamed of everything that is real about us; ashamed of ourselves, of our relatives, of our incomes, of our accents, of our opinions, of our experience, just as we are ashamed of our naked skins.

GEORGE BERNARD SHAW

Y ou've already started dealing with your anxiety by addressing the relationship between your thoughts and emotions; you're learning to express yourself to others. Now it's time to assess how comfortable you are about the way you present yourself in the physical world.

How do you feel about the way you look? Or the way you talk? Or where you live? Or your family background? Or your education?

THE POWER OF SELF-ACCEPTANCE

In a society that seems obsessed with self-improvement, it's difficult not to fixate on our shortcomings. But we can read every self-help book and magazine article, take countless courses on improving personal appearance, learn to eat a healthy diet, work to build strong relationships, and still be devastated by criticism or rejection.

We can practice techniques for self-assertive communication, but no matter how good a particular method is, it can't by itself make us feel understood. The only way to be truly comfortable with others is to be truly comfortable with ourselves.

Being at ease means developing an appreciation for who we really are. Self-esteem comes from knowing and approving of ourselves as unique, valuable beings. None of us are perfect, and none of us are hopelessly flawed.

Our Outward Selves

Accepting the outer aspects of ourselves is part of the process of self-acceptance. It's crucial that we see and approve of all the various elements that make us who we are. When we can't accept certain parts of ourselves, it's difficult to feel good about our whole selves. When we have a realistic view of our strengths and weaknesses, we can appreciate both compliments and criticism, because both contribute to continuing development.

We all have strong feelings about the physical image we project. These are usually expressed through clothes and hairstyles, the fitness and shape of our bodies. And we all have strict models for comparison. Are we too tall, too short, too thin, too fat when compared to our ideal? If our hair is thinning or graying, what does that say about us? Our concepts of beauty and ugliness have enormous impact on our self image.

But physicality is only one part of our identity. Who our parents were, where we were born, where we grew up, where we went to school, how well we did there, what we do in our work, how much money we earn, whether or not we are married, have children, where we live, what our failures or successes have been, what "sins" we've committed, what virtues we personified—pieces of our past that continue to affect our current social interactions.

When we are critical or unforgiving of any personal fault, we feel anxious around others. These negative feelings about ourselves are the generic anxiety we talked about in chapter 1.

We may not recognize that we're experiencing generic anxiety until a particular person, or a situation involving other people, provokes that vague, but unmistakable feeling of discomfort. The dynamics of the situation combined with our negative, unresolved feelings about ourselves cause the symptoms we recognize as social anxiety.

If we react by avoiding people and situations that evoke uneasiness, we condemn ourselves to an anxious existence. If, instead, we stop and examine the roots of our anxiety, we'll quickly learn that our inadequacies, like everything else in life, are relative.

Generic anxiety usually stems from one of three areas of vital concern: appearance, intelligence, and social ability. Most of the compliments and criticisms we receive are related to one or all of them and all three are closely tied to our self-esteem.

We can't help comparing these aspects of ourselves to other people, or to an abstract standard or ideal. We evaluate our appearance by comparing ourself to an advertising company's model; we rank our intelligence on a scale in which genius rates a C+; we analyze our social skills as if we were competing to be Miss Congeniality or the secretary of state.

From the time we're children, we're all susceptible to criticism about these three integral components of our complete self. "Look out, here comes four-eyes," "Quiet, you big dope," and "Watch out, klutz," are common insults but they can strike deep at our self-esteem, often deeper than we realize. When we enter adolescence, our sensitivity about how we appear to others increases dramatically, and continues at a high level throughout our lives—*unless* we consciously learn to accept ourselves.

A GENERIC ANXIETY INVENTORY

Taking an inventory of your generic anxiety will help you recognize which factors in your life cause your discomfort.

Answer as honestly as you can; your reply should indicate how you really feel about yourself. Don't answer the questions based on what you think *others* think about you. If your family is disappointed by your choice of profession, don't try to guess how they would answer the questions about your work. Write down how *you* feel about your job.

Discerning how you really feel might be difficult. You may be unaware how others have influenced your self-image. If friends always tell you that you're great looking, you might respond automatically that you feel fine about your appearance. If someone has made you feel ashamed of your body, you might not know how to appreciate your physical assets.

On the other hand, if you've been told all your life that you're short, but you honestly never have felt short, then don't be afraid to say you feel okay about your height. Try to separate your own feelings from what you've been told. Give the response that matches your inner truth.

THE GENERIC ANXIETY INVENTORY

Rating Scale: Answer each question based on how you feel about yourself.

  0 = Uncomfortable; this is definitely a negative factor.
  1 = Neutral; this doesn't make me feel good, but I can live with it.
  2 = Positive; but this part of me could still use improvement.
  3 = Very Positive; this is one of my strong points.

If I meet someone who wants to know:	I Feel:			
Where I was born	0	1	2	3
Where I grew up	0	1	2	3
Where I went to college	0	1	2	3
How well I did in college	0	1	2	3
What my occupation is	0	1	2	3

Where I've worked in the past	0	1	2	3
How much money I earn	0	1	2	3
How I spend my spare time	0	1	2	3
If I'm seeing anyone special	0	1	2	3
How my marriage is working out	0	1	2	3
How my children are doing	0	1	2	3
What part of town I live in	0	1	2	3
What kind of place I live in	0	1	2	3
What my religion is	0	1	2	3

When I think about:		*I Feel:*		
How my nose looks	0	1	2	3
How my face looks	0	1	2	3
How my hair looks	0	1	2	3
How I style my hair	0	1	2	3
The clothing I usually wear	0	1	2	3
How I look in my clothes	0	1	2	3
How my hands look	0	1	2	3
How my feet look	0	1	2	3
How my body looks	0	1	2	3

My height	0	1	2	3
My weight	0	1	2	3
My posture	0	1	2	3
My state of health	0	1	2	3
My ability to converse with others	0	1	2	3
My ability to entertain others	0	1	2	3
My ability to relate to others	0	1	2	3
My ability to get along with others	0	1	2	3
My ability to understand others	0	1	2	3
My education	0	1	2	3
My job training	0	1	2	3
My experience with the world	0	1	2	3
My ability to earn money	0	1	2	3
My ability to raise my children	0	1	2	3
My contribution to the world	0	1	2	3

EVALUATING YOUR INVENTORY

If you find that you answered just as many questions on the inventory with 0s and 1s as you did with 2s and 3s, you're in good company. Most people have some aspects of themselves that make them feel confident and others that cause anxiety.

If most of your answers were 2s or 3s, go back and ask yourself if you were being honest about your feelings. Sometimes, higher scores mean you're not yet aware of the source of your anxiety.

If you found yourself answering a majority of questions with 0s and 1s, you're acknowledging your generic anxiety. Instead of worrying that you have lots of problem areas, congratulate yourself on your awareness of your true thoughts and feelings.

Go back to any questions you answered with a 0 or a 1, and make specific notes about that aspect of yourself. For example, if you don't feel good about your ability to converse with others, what exactly is your problem? Do you have trouble speaking, do you stutter, or do you find it difficult to make yourself heard? Maybe you feel that your vocabulary is inadequate. Or maybe you know lots of words, but you can't pronounce them properly.

If you have an accent, you might worry that people make fun of you. Maybe you just don't like the sound of your voice. Are you too loud, too nasal, or too whiney? The more details you can list, the easier it will be to address your generic anxiety.

One of the reasons that generic anxiety is so pervasive is that we avoid thinking about anything that makes us uncomfortable. Becoming fully conscious of our anxiety by writing down our thoughts and feelings helps us gain a realistic perspective. So, be persistent!

A REALISTIC ASSESSMENT

How did you answer the inventory questions about your work life? If you rated yourself less than 3, ask yourself what standard you are using to evaluate yourself.

It's okay to judge yourself based on your criteria for success but not to measure yourself on some impossible yardstick of excellence.

Realistic Assessment: George

George works in the reference department of a large city library. Despite the wealth of information he processes every day, George feels insecure in almost all social situations. By his own evaluation, he is isolated in an ivory tower of arcane knowledge and completely ignorant about what goes on in what he considers the real world.

George can't help comparing himself to the people he admires most, the newscasters on television and the foreign correspondents for the *New York Times*. George feels hopeless, because at the age of forty-five, he knows it's impossible for him to accomplish as much as the media professionals he holds in such high regard.

George judges his ability to converse with other people, to entertain others, to relate to others, and to understand the world not in terms of his own life, but in terms of an abstract ideal. His absolute assumptions about what he *should* know are a form of generalizing. In his distorted view, he ought to be as aware of the news as people whose jobs demand that they keep abreast of world events.

George may admire reporters and broadcasters, but he has no real *need* to know the intricacies of world events. As a librarian, he comes across more interesting facts every day than most people encounter in a year. If his goal is to become more comfortable with social interactions, George could use his own work as a starting point for some interesting conversations.

On the other hand it's possible that by paying attention to his discomfort, George has discovered a real need to involve himself with the understanding of world events. If he looks at his situation realistically, George may see some solutions. He could take courses on current events, or travel, or spend time reading in depth about political issues.

Depending on his other skills and how much effort he devoted to his interest, George might be able to find a full-time job that would fulfill his dream. Even if he never becomes a television reporter or a journalist, he might use his library experience to get a research position with a political organization, think tank, or news publication.

The important step for George is realizing that he creates his anxiety by measuring his achievements against an unrealistic, impractical standard. When he knows that the source of his social discomfort is an unwillingness to accept himself, he can spend some time evaluating his options.

But What If My Problem Is Permanent?

Even when our generic anxiety stems from a physical characteristic that cannot be changed, we can learn to reevaluate our thinking about ourselves.

Realistic Assessment: Gloria

Gloria felt very uncomfortable about the size of her hands. She answered the inventory question about hands with a 0, then went back and wrote these notes: "My hands are too big. All my life I've been self-conscious about them. When I'm talking with other people, my hands make me feel out of place and ugly."

Questioning basic assumptions by asking what is provoking our anxious feelings usually reveals the thought distortions behind those feelings. Gloria's anxiety was focused on a physical characteristic but like George, she was a victim of absolute thinking in using an idealistic standard to measure herself. She felt her hands were too big, but she never stopped to ask herself why she felt this way.

Is there a standard for hand size? Was Gloria comparing her hands with someone else's? Why did she think her hands were too big? Did she have a job that required her to fit her hands into tiny places? Was it her secret dream to be a glove model? Or maybe she wanted to do detergent commercials on television? Could she name even one thing that her hands were too big to do?

When Gloria began to think about her hands realistically, she realized that her old concern no longer felt important.

Maybe her hands were a little bigger than most people's but this was not a problem on which she wanted to expend any more energy. She came up with some ideas to help her feel better about her hands.

> I don't know why I've been so obsessed with my hands. What a bizarre thing to worry about. I should feel grateful that I have two hands. Maybe someone criticized them, and I accepted it without thinking. I don't know. But I know one thing, instead of trying to measure my hands (my self?) against everyone else's, from now on, I'm just going to take care of them. I'll treat myself to a manicure to remind myself that I'm in great shape.

JOURNAL EXERCISE # 1

This exercise will show you how to use realistic thinking to address your generic anxiety. Remember to be as specific as you can and to look for patterns in your responses.

1. Go back over your generic anxiety inventory. For every question you answered 0 or 1, make a note of the real issue that makes you feel anxious. For example, if you feel uncomfortable about your hair, what is it about your hair that bothers you?

2. Now ask yourself some realistic questions, focusing on what is really at stake. If thinning hair makes you feel anxious, ask yourself what thin hair means to you. What does your thinning hair say about you as a person? Why are you uncomfortable with that?

3. Make some notes for dealing with your anxiety and for addressing your concern. If thinning hair makes you feel unhealthy, you could see a specialist. If thinning hair makes you realize you're aging, why are you uncomfortable about getting older?

Here are some examples from the journals of people who took the Generic Anxiety Inventory.

MARGARET'S JOURNAL

I feel uncomfortable about my thinning hair.

What is the real problem? What does it mean when hair thins? Am I aging prematurely? Is this a family trait? Maybe I have some disease? Will my friends disown me? Will my husband expect me to wear a wig? My thinning hair makes me feel inadequate! What can I do to feel better? I could go to a doctor, to be sure that nothing's wrong with me. I could try a different hairstyle, maybe get a permanent, so my hair doesn't look so thin. If it makes me feel more attractive, I could even wear a hairpiece.

I can also practice separating myself from my hair. I am a whole lot more than hair. I really don't think my husband would love me less if I were bald. I think I'll ask him.

ED'S JOURNAL

Problem: I'm not comfortable with my height. I've always been too short.

Feelings: When the other guys started getting taller in high school, I started feeling left out. College was worse. And so is work. People don't take you seriously when you're the shortest man on the staff. It makes me feel inadequate when women look down on me.

Realistic questions: I feel like women look down on me, but do they really? And do the people I work with really think less of me because of my height? How would my life be different if I were taller?

A new look at myself: My wife is short, and I fell in love with her. She's a wonderful, attractive, sensuous woman, and her height doesn't detract from that at all.

I used to dream about being a pilot, but I was too short for the Air Force. If I really wanted to fly, I could take lessons on a private plane, where there are no height requirements.

Resolutions: I've been blaming my problems on other people's attitudes, when it's really my own attitude that's causing my anxiety. I'd feel much better if I stopped assuming that I know what other people are thinking.

LYNDA'S JOURNAL

What I don't like about myself: I'm overweight!

How do I feel about it? I hate it, and I hate myself because of it. My clothes don't fit anymore. I always look awful.

What does being fat mean to me? It means I'm unable to take care of myself properly. It means something is wrong with me. People think I'm a lazy slob, even though I work as hard as they do.

Am I being realistic? Not entirely. I don't know what other people think, that's mind-reading. And I'm also generalizing, by making the absolute assumption that if I'm overweight, then I'm inadequate as a person.

But my weight is real. I weigh sixty pounds more than my doctor says I should. And the weight affects my health as well as my self-esteem.

What could I do? I could change my eating habits and start exercising. If I can't do it by myself, I could join Overeaters Anonymous or Weight Watchers. And I can spend more time working on my feelings, because there's probably a reason why I've let myself get in such bad shape.

When Lynda began to use her journal, she was amazed to see how much energy she spent avoiding the cause of her anxiety. It was much easier to blame herself and others for the way she felt than to look realistically at her weight problem. Obesity is a serious health condition and something Lynda was able to change, once she faced it.

Lynda continued working with her journal and joined a health club diet program. She found that sharing her problems with others helped her feel better about herself, and her improved self-esteem helped with her efforts to lose weight.

THE EYE OF THE BEHOLDER

Every month hundreds of articles appear in popular magazines telling us how to look, how to dress, how to wear our hair, and how to change our personality. It's tempting to believe that with a few adjustments we can become somehow perfect. But it rarely turns out that beauty tricks or communication strategies solve any problems. Ultimately, we have to ask ourselves who we are trying to please.

Have you ever wondered why there is so much pressure on all of us, men and women, to look like the models in magazines? Have you ever questioned the ideas of beauty those models represent? Although the means of persuasion have become more sophisticated in the last century, the message is as old as time.

Beginning with the earliest folktales and legends, goodness has been personified in the beautiful princess who wins the handsome prince. In mythology and children's stories, evil is symbolized by the ugly old witch or the scary old bogeyman. Advertising sells the same message: if we're young and beautiful, then we're good, and we deserve to live happily ever after.

This pattern of distorted thinking is called *twisted logic*. In real life, beauty does not determine someone's goodness. And whether we fit someone else's standard of beauty has nothing to do with whether we deserve a happy life.

But legends and advertising still exert a powerful pull on us. Whether consciously or not, we draw conclusions based on how other people look and act. We have our own ideas about physical attractiveness, but we also get cues from other people's gestures and nonverbal expressions. The way people move, their posture, their body language, all communicate messages we either accept or reject. Even subtle, subconscious responses like blinking and breathing can influence how we see others and how we are seen by others.

APPEARANCE ATTITUDE SURVEY

Answer "true" or "false" to the following questions. Be as honest as possible about your own experiences.

1. Trim, well-dressed women advance in their jobs faster than women who are overweight.

2. Thin people are more high-strung than heavy-set people.

3. Overweight people are undisciplined.

4. Male executives who dye their hair make a quick climb up the corporate ladder, while men the same age who leave their hair gray stay in unsatisfactory positions a few years longer.

5. Brunettes are more serious than blondes.

6. It is not how intelligent we are that gets us ahead in life, but how intelligent we appear to others.

7. Dark-skinned people are sexier than fair-skinned people.

8. Management-level and higher positions require a certain degree of grace and social expertise.

9. Balding men are more virile than men with all their hair.

10. Men with all their hair are more virile than balding men.

Evaluating Your Attitude

If you answered "true" to any of the questions, your experiences have taught you that appearances do count. We are all influenced by appearances, whether we are aware of it or not, whether we want to be or not.

Appearances serve social functions, even when we're not

consciously aware of their importance. We recognize members of the police department, the fire department, and the post office by their uniforms. We wouldn't trust a surgeon who didn't wear a scrub-suit into surgery, and we might think twice about investing our money in a bank if its president came to work dressed in torn blue-jeans.

Presenting a nice appearance is important to most people, but what *is* nice? For many of us, an acceptable appearance means that we conform, expressing only conventional choices in order to please others. But how can we ever really know what will please others?

No matter what strategy we use, no matter how much effort we put into fitting in, we can never control someone else's perceptions about us. In fact, the more we try to please others, the more we feel manipulated.

The alternative is to accept ourselves as we are. Instead of frustrating ourselves by trying to please others, we can experience the satisfaction of pleasing ourselves.

THE SECRET OF SELF-IMPROVEMENT

Some people give up on themselves when they realize that they can't guarantee a desired benefit by dressing or acting a certain way. If the only reason you want to improve yourself is to manipulate others, you'll never experience the real benefit of self-improvement.

Appearance and Self-Improvement: Mary

Mary was very serious about her career in market research. She was intelligent and had a business degree, but at promotion time she lost out to the men in her department. Then a friend who was a successful stockbroker suggested that Mary try dressing in a more business-like style. "I don't like wearing suits, either," the friend confessed, "but it's essential for my job."

Mary read several books on dressing for success and

began to believe that her long hair and flower-print dresses were creating the wrong image in her office environment. She had her hair cut into a short, more serious style. And because "career clothes" seemed so important, Mary spent a small fortune on expensive suits and designer blouses, even though the outfits felt stiff and uncomfortable.

But after two years, Mary still had not gotten a promotion. Instead of feeling good about her efforts, she felt trapped, because she was always trying to fit herself into an image of the perfect research analyst.

Mary began to feel more and more uncomfortable with her own appearance. Her dark business suits made her feel she was using her appearance to manipulate others. She found herself increasingly unable to be herself.

Initially Mary thought that her situation at work made her anxious, but she began to realize that her anxiety was more about herself than about the people who had failed to promote her career. After spending a few weeks trying to understand her feelings, Mary acknowledged that she was dissatisfied with the type of work she was doing.

She had been hoping that a promotion would make her feel better about herself, but now she could see that getting ahead was not what she really wanted. Instead of spending her time analyzing how packaging affected purchases, she wanted to do something to make people's lives better. Mary finally understood that her efforts to change her appearance had been "Band-aids." She had been avoiding herself by focusing on her clothes.

The most important aspect of self-improvement is that the need to improve come from within. If we consciously or unconsciously try to please others, our efforts cannot increase our self-esteem. Mary's efforts had unhappy results, not because of choices she made, but because the reasons for her choices lay outside herself. In wearing suits that seemed to fit the image of the perfect market analyst, Mary was trying to please others, not herself.

Author Charles Hix explains in *Dressing Right* that our clothing is an extension of our personalities. Although we won't gain social confidence by dressing in a certain way, appearance *is* a real component in social interaction. When we're confident about ourselves, our clothing sends out that message.

When You're At Your Best
The real secret of self-improvement is knowing what makes you look and feel your best and then emphasizing it. Beauty is a composite of features and style. Very few people are perfect; most people who seem so are good at emphasizing their strong points.

If you're not sure how to point up your strengths, you might ask the opinion of an expert. A consultation with a dermatologist or a cosmetic surgeon can help you make realistic decisions before you begin any program for modifying your appearance. A good fashion consultant, make-up artist, or hair stylist can give you advice based on your specific beauty needs. Nutrition and exercise specialists can help you design a physical fitness program. Don't overlook the free advice from department store consultants or the staff at your local health club.

Another important resource is your bookstore or library. Self-improvement books can help, once you've made your own decision to do something about a particular weak point. Consciously acknowledging a problem area often creates a strong desire for change.

Frustrated, Mary decided to look for a new job. She found one with a nonprofit organization that could use her business skills. As a reward to herself, she made an appointment with a fashion consultant. The consultant described a different concept of dressing for success: understanding yourself and knowing what makes you comfortable, so you can project an image of competence.

Mary had already tried the traditional business look and wasn't happy with it. She had given up her individual style because she wanted to fit in. The consultant suggested developing a third style, one that combined a traditional business look with Mary's favorite florals.

The next time Mary went shopping she bought clothes that would be appropriate for work, but also suited her personal taste. She also found that with her new sense of accomplishment, she felt no need to overspend.

Working with the consultant helped Mary understand the connection between her feelings and her choice of clothing. What changed was not just Mary's style, but her attitude about herself. She accepted and approved of her own taste and that gave her a renewed self-confidence. Mary wasn't even surprised when six months later she was promoted at her new job. Her success in getting along with others was cited as a real benefit to her department.

COMPETENCE

We wouldn't ask an architect to train our dog. We don't want our dentist to plead our case in court or hang our track lighting. It's okay for *other* people to be limited in their skills or highly qualified in one particular area, but we have higher expectations for ourselves—we want to do it all! When we can't, we feel incompetent.

Gaining expertise in one field means letting go of many others. You might be musically gifted, but unable to learn foreign languages, or you might be a prize-winning poet who can't balance your checkbook, and this makes you feel incompetent.

But competence does not mean excelling at everything. Competence means appreciating your talents, and knowing when you need help. When you recognize your own special qualities, skills and accomplishments, you'll find it no longer matters what other people expect of you.

JOURNAL EXERCISE #2

This exercise will help you recognize and appreciate your unique talents.

1. Make a list of anything you have ever done that made you feel good about yourself. Put down anything, no matter how big or how small. Include even successes that only you know about.

2. Begin to keep a file on your accomplishments. Make notes and keep little mementos to remind yourself of any little thing that happens that makes you feel good.

The following examples from other people's journals might surprise you, especially if you're not recognizing the wide scope of your innate talents and accomplishments.

FIELDS OF COMPETENCE

Betty's Journal

I'm an expert at running a home. I can organize shopping, cooking, and cleaning for myself and my family. I love telling bedtime stories. I created special stories for my own children, and now my grandchildren love to hear them.

Ed's Journal

I can tell a good joke, and I can make a lousy joke interesting. I have a knack for making people laugh. I help them forget their problems.

Mary's Journal

No matter what's in the refrigerator, I can whip up a fantastic dinner. I'm very creative with food, especially with pasta sauces.

George's Journal

I'm a trivia expert. One of my special interests is boxing. I started writing a column, now I do television commentary on current matches. My show is popular because I offer my viewers history, statistics, and interesting anecdotes.

Gloria's Journal

I'm good at languages, and I taught myself to speak sign language. I volunteer at a local school for deaf children.

ACCOMPLISHMENT FILES

Sara's Journal

I once convinced a single mother I knew to finish high school. The last time I saw her, she was working as a nurse and supporting her son.

Margaret's Journal

I made an appointment to see a specialist about my thinning hair. It doesn't sound like a big deal, but feeling free to talk about my secret fear was quite a feat for me.

Marsha's Journal

I have a letter from a woman who was once my secretary. Her letter thanks me for the enjoyable work experience and for letting her know how important her help was to my success.

STATUS CONSCIOUSNESS

Some people are snobs. They are status conscious, which means they view the world through a series of labels. If you went to the "right" university, if you live in the "right" part of town, if you drive the "right" car, they consider you a satisfactory person. It's easy to feel self-conscious when someone evaluates your life using these superficial labels, instead of asking what you've learned, what you're capable of doing, and what kind of person you are.

Status anxiety usually results when we contrast our achievements with the success of others. We feel awkward around people who make more money, drive bigger cars, and wear more expensive clothes. Our anxiety may be compounded by insecurities about our jobs, salaries, and material possessions, but the basic cause of our discomfort is low self-esteem.

When we accept ourselves, we feel valuable. When we approve of ourselves, we can appreciate our efforts without needing to compare ourselves to others. We can look forward to higher achievements and accomplishments while still appreciating who we are and what we have now.

SOCIAL RULES

Manners that are obligatory at certain social functions, often called social etiquette, can seem mysterious to the uninitiated. When it comes to this particular stylized behavior, idiosyncracies flourish. As philosopher Joseph Wood Krutch wrote in *The Modern Temper*, "There is no conceivable human action [that] custom has not at one time justified and at another condemned."

Say you're eating with friends in a Chinese restaurant, and you're the only one who doesn't know how to use chopsticks. Or you're the only Christian at the bar mitzvah of your boss's son. Whether you're moving to a new place, starting a new job, or attending a function you're not familiar with, the way to feel comfortable is to look at the situation realistically and accept yourself.

If you don't know the proper behavior, there's no reason you can't admit that and learn. Ask yourself if your anxiety is really about etiquette, or about admitting that you're a novice. No one is expected to know how to do something the first time. In fact, there is a charm to beginners who are open and willing to learn. Asking for help is a good way to break through nervousness and meet someone new. And quite often, when you admit that you don't know what to do, other people will admit that they don't, either.

JOURNAL EXERCISE #3

This exercise will help you focus on your strengths and accept your weaknesses.

    1. Make a realistic evaluation of your strong points and your weak points. To start, you might look back at your answers in the generic anxiety inventory earlier in this chapter.

    2. How can you make the most of your good points and de-emphasize your weak points?

    3. Can you direct your own efforts, or should you seek professional advice and help?

The following examples might help you get started.

CARL'S JOURNAL

Weak point: My appearance. I'm fairly smart, a hard worker, and good instructor. But I'm too tall and gangly. I can't hide, because I'm so tall. And I'm a history teacher, not a basketball player.

Emphasize: My charming personality! I really am a nice person, and I have good friends. I should concentrate on that and not worry about my height.

De-emphasize: My not-so-great coordination. I'm just not a sport and field type. I am, however, great at verbal jousting. I should look for people who appreciate me for what I am.

Could I get help? Maybe. I could take a dance class, and see if there's any hope for improvement. Of course I'd have to be willing to look clumsy while I'm learning, but maybe it would be worth it. Maybe it would even be fun!

JONAH'S JOURNAL

My good points: I'm a hard worker, and I love my work. I'm great at analysis, I'm very organized, and I'm careful with details.

My weak point: I still don't have an MBA, so I'm on the bottom of the promotion list.

I like people, but I have a hard time being sociable. I get bored with chit-chat. I know that if I could be more friendly, my degree problem wouldn't seem so formidable.

Emphasize: To make the most of my work skills, I can continue doing a good job. Maybe I could talk to my boss about the possibility of going back to school. I don't need an MBA, but all the people who move up have the degree. Maybe I could go to school at night. And if I talk about my concerns, my boss will know I'm serious about my career.

De-emphasize: I can't bury my inability to socialize, unless I just avoid everyone. I guess the only answer is to try to get to know more people so I won't feel like being sociable is such a chore. Or maybe I could find something to do with other people that I would really enjoy, like playing cards or chess.

What I can do: I can take care of talking with my boss. But I'm not sure how to go about being more outgoing and friendly. I think I need to learn how to really talk to people, so I don't get stuck in useless conversations.

THE IMPORTANCE OF CONVERSATION

Whether we're acquainting ourselves with a new culture or familiarizing ourselves with our everyday world, whether we're learning to know our colleagues better or trying to meet people in our new neighborhood, nothing will help as much as the ability to start and maintain a conversation. The anxiety that comes up when we're unable to converse with others is often enough to make us avoid future interactions. Yet, as Psychologist Jonathan Cheek, Ph.D., explains in *Conquering Shyness,* what we actually need is more interaction, so we can practice talking with others.

We've learned that practicing makes us more comfortable expressing our feelings. The same is true for social conversation. The more we interact, the more comfortable it feels. When we realize that we *can* have an enjoyable conversation, even with people we don't know well, we begin to enjoy doing it, so we do it more often.

Talking comfortably with others is a large part of feeling at ease in social interactions. When we feel good about our ability to communicate, we feel good about ourselves, too.

CONVERSATION STRATEGIES

If conversing with others is difficult for you, try some of the following approaches.

Be Genuine. One problem with forcing ourselves into conversations is that we feel we must keep the conversation going, no matter what. Try to think of any conversation opportunity as a way to get to know someone, or to know someone better.

Be Personal. Ask questions you'd really like to know the answer to. You may not want to intrude, but being polite doesn't mean you can't get personal. Most people like to be asked how they feel about an issue, because it means you value their experience.

Focus on the Other Person's Words. When you're feeling anxious, you're probably thinking about anything other than the conversation you're trying to have. Listening to the other person will take your mind off yourself. Try to register every word the other person says, and ask for an explanation if you don't understand the meaning of something.

Practice. If you have concerns about the way you speak, you might want to practice with a tape recorder, a drama class, or a speech coach.

JOURNAL EXERCISE #4

This exercise will help you practice your conversation skills.

1. Try to start a conversation with a stranger—perhaps someone you see in an elevator, someone at the grocery store, or someone walking your way on the street, or waiting at your bus stop.

2. Try maintaining a conversation by saying something you ordinarily might withhold. See if you can learn something you don't already know.

3. Notice the difference in the way you talk with different people. Do you pay closer attention to your friends, or to strangers?

4. Notice how you feel after each conversation. Can you appreciate the efforts you've made? How can you improve future conversations?

6 AT EASE WITH YOUR BODY

We all know the experience of anxiety, the constriction in the chest and throat, the pounding heart, the inner sinking—the feeling of imminent chaos and utter destruction . . . Except in the smallest of doses it is overwhelming.

ERNEST BECKER
The Birth and Death of Meaning

Reason can wrestle and overthrow terror.

EURIPIDES

What happens to your body when anxiety strikes? Do you tremble or blush? Does your heart seem to race, or pound in your chest? Do you become suddenly cold and shiver, or do you begin to sweat profusely? Maybe your stomach is affected, and you feel queasy or nauseous?

You may be all too familiar with the unpleasant physical symptoms of anxiety. You may spend a lot of time and energy avoiding people and situations that trigger these physical responses. But have you ever stopped to think why your body responds to stress in this way?

Where do the physical symptoms of anxiety originate? Are they caused by chemical changes in your body? Is one genetically predisposed to them or are these reactions programmed during infancy and childhood?

As philosopher Ernest Becker explains in *The Birth and Death of Meaning,* these questions have been the subject of continuing debate between psychoanalysts and behavioral psychologists since Freud and Adler first asked them. What we do know is that social anxiety has many possible origins. Even if we can't determine a precise cause, we can benefit from understanding the subtle interplay of many contributing factors.

Social anxiety usually develops after a series of injuries to the psyche. Years of exposures and reactions may build up before we consciously recognize an anxiety response. Even after we've learned to identify problems with our identity and self-esteem, our physical symptoms don't necessarily disappear.

But we can bring about change. We can learn how physical responses interact with thoughts and feelings, and how negative emotions can lead to negative physical reactions. As we change our inner reality and adopt realistic and positive mental and emotional outlooks, we can also learn to manage our physical reactions.

THE PHYSIOLOGICAL RESPONSE

Even before we become aware of any physical reaction to stress, our body has already made a series of involuntary adjustments. Our neck muscles stiffen, our breathing becomes shallow or we hold our breath too long, the major muscles in our bodies contract or tighten. By the time we notice that our palms are sweating, we're at the mercy of our physiological state.

Anxiety is associated with chemical changes in our brain. Some of the changes are survival mechanisms we've inherited from our primitive ancestors. Without any conscious action on our parts, our sympathetic nervous system reacts to a perceived threat by releasing epinephrine and norepinephrine into various parts of the body and by stimulating the adrenal gland to release epinephrine into the bloodstream.

These hormones cause obvious physiological changes: the heart beats quicker and harder, air passages widen and breathing quickens, blood vessels in the muscles dilate, while blood vessels in the gastrointestinal system and skin contract. The sympathetic nervous system is preparing the body for self-defense, making it possible to respond by either fighting or fleeing, which is why the process is known as the *fight or flight response.*

We've all heard stories about ninety-pound grandmothers who lift automobiles to save children trapped underneath. We know that under deadline pressure, nothing helps like "getting the adrenaline pumping." Neurotransmitters make miracles possible, but problems occur when a stress reaction is inappropriate to the situation. Unfortunately, the brain message center that triggers the sympathetic nervous system can't always distinguish a real threat from an imaginary one.

Think about what happens when you watch a scary movie. Your muscles tense, your mouth feels dry, your palms become moist. Or you suddenly feel cold and your whole body begins to tremble. Your breathing and heart rate are fast, and grow faster as the events on the screen become more and more terrifying. Then the monster jumps out of hiding, fangs dripping with blood. You scream!

In reality, you are sitting in a dark room, safe from any danger. But your brain's reality is that danger is real, so it stimulated your fight or flight response. When the movie is over, you may be drained or exhausted, even though you haven't moved. What you're feeling are the aftereffects of ninety minutes of stress.

The same physiological chain of events operates when we're anxious at the prospect of a stressful encounter. Just thinking about calling someone for a date, or considering going to a party alone, or anticipating an important job interview may be enough to stimulate a stress reaction.

When thoughts and feelings are distorted, the physical response to anxiety is increased. Attempts to avoid our symptoms cause their own stress and ultimately we can be trapped in a spiral of suffering.

The Physiological Response: Harriet

Harriet excelled in her college English courses, and expected to become a playwright. After graduation she got a job assisting a well-known producer. Her career was derailed when she met and married the leading actor in one of the plays she helped produce. Over the next few years, she found it difficult to focus on herself or her own plans.

When her husband had some financial success, Harriet finally decided to make the plunge. She quit her job and stayed at home to write. After several months, she made an appointment to show her work to a producer.

The meeting didn't go as well as Harriet had hoped. As the producer pointed out the parts of the play that he felt should be rewritten, Harriet found herself feeling flushed and warm. The feeling progressed until she had difficulty breathing. She felt as if she were going to faint.

Harriet's symptoms were so severe that she saw her doctor. He explained that she was suffering the physical effects of anxiety. Harriet understood that her feelings of inadequacy were triggered by the meeting with the producer, but she thought the only answer was to write a play good enough to be produced. Instead of getting better, Harriet found that every time she showed her work to someone, she had a similar reaction.

As Harriet was preparing to meet with an actor who had agreed to read her play, she began to feel the back of her neck getting warm. She panicked, expecting that her usual symptoms would soon follow. As she rushed to the telephone to cancel her appointment, her hand went instinctively to the back of her neck, where she found the hot curlers she had put in her hair earlier.

Harriet's experience may seem humorous, but for her it was a turning point. She understood for the first time that her stress response resulted from her feelings and thoughts about herself, not from someone's reaction to her work. That realization was enough for Harriet to get serious about dealing with her sense of inadequacy.

Most anxiety reactions are related to thoughts and feelings, fantasies and fears. But some illnesses or substances can cause chemical reactions that we may interpret as symptoms of anxiety. In *The Good News About Panic, Anxiety, and Phobias,* Dr. Mark Gold cites more than forty illnesses that may be culprits, including such diverse disorders as hyperthyroidism, diabetes, temporal-lobe epilepsy, mononucleosis, niacin deficiency, and heart attacks.

Physical reactions to sugar and caffeine that resemble symptoms of anxiety are well-recognized, but not many people know they may experience severe reactions after exposure to environmental chemicals, including household cleaning products, inks, dyes, and pesticides. In her book, *Nontoxic, Natural & Earthwise,* Debra Lynn Dadd describes the reactions people can develop to chemicals found in ordinary home and work products. Physical symptoms resulting from allergy, toxic chemical exposure or hypersensitivity to more benign chemicals can mimic the symptoms of anxiety. Reactions to external factors, especially when we don't know their source may create their own feelings of anxiety, or aggravate anxiety that's already present. The more we learn about our own physical responses, the more control we can exert over our lives.

How Can I Tell Internal from External?

If your anxiety is a sudden, recent problem, you might benefit from a careful assessment of your enviornment. Are you using more sugar or caffeine than before? Is your car emitting any unusual fumes or smoke? Have you recently bought new carpeting, or painted your apartment or varnished furniture? Even doing too much exercise can stimulate an anxiety reaction, as can sitting in front of a computer screen under fluorescent lights.

If you suspect that any factor contributing to your anxiety might be physical, schedule an appointment with your family physician. Take whatever steps are necessary to find and eliminate the problem right away.

For most of us, the source of anxiety will be found within our minds. Even when our most obvious, troublesome symptom seems to be physical, effective treatment has to focus on developing our sense of identity and self-esteem. We have to learn to approve of ourselves, including the part that reacts physically to social anxiety.

GENETIC CONTROLS VERSUS BEHAVIORAL MODELS

The question of whether we inherit a predisposition to anxiety or learn the anxiety response as children is irrelevant to understanding the meaning of anxiety in our lives. Whether influenced by biochemical factors or by learning, our symptoms are reactions to inner fears. Knowing the cause of anxiety doesn't automatically change its effect on us or our reaction to it.

We do know that anxiety, like depression and alcoholism, tends to occur in families. But even if we someday discover a specific gene for this susceptibility, we still may not solve the controversy. Childhood experiences are so important to psychological development that we may never be able to distinguish the genetic from environmental influences.

The way our families and significant people in our lives respond to social encounters establishes an early blueprint for our own behavior and our concept of who we are. But sometimes the identities and behavior patterns we develop are reactions *against* our role models.

Behavior Models: Bobby

Bobby was an introverted child, born into an extroverted family. Because they were all loud and outgoing, Bobby's parents and brothers and sisters regarded him as something of an oddball.

Bobby was quiet and preferred staying at home. To "cure" Bobby, his parents pushed him to go to parties and sporting events. But Bobby reacted by trembling and sweating. At one point, he almost fainted, which embarrassed his parents.

His parent's reaction made the situation worse. The

more Bobby resisted, the more they pushed. By the time he was seventeen, Bobby had a severe case of social anxiety that continued until he had to seek help as an adult.

Families like Bobby's believe that being different is a negative factor that requires change. The child is forced into situations as if they were tests. Can the child put aside his different behavior and act like everyone else?

Bobby was not given any tools for dealing with new and difficult situations. His parents could have suggested ways to talk to the other children at a party, or they could have explained that it was natural for him to feel uncomfortable in a new situation around people he didn't know very well. Instead, he was expected to perform according to his parent's model, not his own. His parents and their other children enjoyed parties, so they assumed Bobby would do the same.

When Bobby recognized his parent's disappointment and disapproval, he equated difference with being inadequate. His self-esteem and self-confidence was diminished, and he decided that the only way to protect himself was to avoid similar situations whenever possible.

Behavior Models: Pamela

Pamela was a musically gifted child, and her parents frequently asked her to give piano recitals at their parties. Performing in front of an audience was difficult for her. She became nervous and forgot passages she had known well.

Pamela's mother sympathized, since she had experienced much the same feelings as a girl. But her parents had insisted that "practice makes perfect," and eventually, Pamela's mother had adapted to the stress of performing.

It was more difficult for Pamela. Her love for music led her to an expensive music school, but she was unable to perform even before her peers. Her symptoms became so severe that she felt nauseous whenever she tried to force herself on stage. Pamela put aside her musical talent to work behind the scenes, becoming the "quiet one" who staged performances for other "more gifted" students.

Instead of helping Pamela find a comfortable way to develop her talent, her parents tried to make her fit their expectations. Because her mother had overcome her own feelings of anxiety, she expected Pamela to do the same. Pamela may have been born with a genetic tendency toward anxiety, but being pushed to perform even when it was clearly traumatic was definitely a factor in the development of her anxiety response.

Pamela's mother reinforced the negative learning she endured as a child, without stopping to ask herself what her own experience had cost and what price she expected her daughter to pay. Despite the importance Pam's mother placed on performing, she herself had given up music, and eventually so did Pamela.

In his book, *Shyness,* psychologist Dr. Philip Zimbardo warns that blaming anxiety on genetics makes people feel that they're incapable of change. Being born with a sensitive nervous system or into a critical family only contributes to our essential anxiety. To deal with anxiety, we have to be willing to change.

The behavioral model offers a more positive approach to change. A large part of social anxiety is a habit, a conditioned reaction to certain stimuli. And habits can be broken! Through a process called behavior modification, any learned response can be unlearned.

TAKING AN INVENTORY

Before you begin a program to modify your physical and behavioral responses to anxiety, you need a clear understanding of your individual pattern of reactions. Do you know exactly what symptoms you experience? Do you know how intense each symptom is in relationship to others? This Inventory of Physical and Behavioral Symptoms of Social Anxiety will help you recognize your response patterns.

Answer each question as honestly as possible. Try to remember how you feel when you are the *most* anxious and uncomfortable. It may help to recall an unpleasant experience, so you can think about how you felt and behaved.

Your physical and behavioral symptoms may be severe, even incapacitating, but you can learn to recognize the factors that trigger them. When you know what causes your reactions, you can begin to desensitize yourself so you no longer have counter-productive responses. You can also teach yourself new, more realistic, and productive ways to respond.

THE SOCIAL ANXIETY BEHAVIOR INVENTORY

Rating Scale: Answer each question based on how you feel during your *worst* anxiety experiences.

    0 = Rarely, or never experienced
    1 = Occasionally experienced, or only a mild sensation
    2 = Frequently experienced, or moderately
        uncomfortable
    3 = Always experienced, symptoms are severe

When I'm anxious:	How often or how severe?			
My skin feels flushed, like I'm blushing.	0	1	2	3
My knees and legs feel weak, shaky.	0	1	2	3
My arms and legs actually tremble and twitch; I can't control them.	0	1	2	3
I feel very clumsy and awkward.	0	1	2	3

I fidget in my chair, or play with any object nearby, including my hair.	0	1	2	3
My throat feels dry; I feel like I have to swallow.	0	1	2	3
My voice breaks up.	0	1	2	3
I stammer, and lose concentration.	0	1	2	3
My speech becomes slurred, and I can't re-member important words.	0	1	2	3
I feel frozen, like I can't move.	0	1	2	3
I cross my arms and legs, but can't make myself comfortable.	0	1	2	3
I can't look at the per-son I'm talking to; I have to avert my eyes.	0	1	2	3
I find myself holding my breath.	0	1	2	3
I feel like I can't catch my breath, like I'm panting or hyperventilating.	0	1	2	3
My heartbeat becomes very fast or irregular.	0	1	2	3
My heart feels like it's pounding in my chest.	0	1	2	3

I can't concentrate or anything, whether I'm talking or someone is talking to me.	0	1	2	3
My ears ring; I hear a buzzing sound.	0	1	2	3
My vision gets blurry.	0	1	2	3
I feel dizzy, like I'm going to faint.	0	1	2	3
I actually faint.	0	1	2	3
My stomach becomes tight and queasy.	0	1	2	3
My stomach gurgles and churns; I feel like I have to go to the bathroom.	0	1	2	3
I feel nauseous.	0	1	2	3
I actually vomit.	0	1	2	3
I feel hot.	0	1	2	3
I perspire.	0	1	2	3
I feel cold.	0	1	2	3
My fingers and feet become cold, or numb and tingling.	0	1	2	3
My head, neck, and shoulders become tense, stiff, or tight.	0	1	2	3
My head feels tight, or it throbs.	0	1	2	3
I eat or smoke compulsively.	0	1	2	3

| I laugh and giggle inappropriately. | 0 | 1 | 2 | 3 |

Evaluating Your Symptoms

Look back at your scores on the inventory. Do your highest scores seem to be related? Or do you have just one symptom that rates a 3? You might want to list your symptoms according to their severity.

Most people experience a range of mild to moderate symptoms. But whether your symptoms are noticeable to other people or not, you might feel them as moderately uncomfortable or severe. Even one severe symptom can make you feel as if you have no control over your body. That desperate awareness, in turn, creates an even greater feeling of anxiety and an intensification of your physical response.

The goal of behavioral modification is to gain control over your body's response to anxiety. When you know that you can manage the physical and behavioral symptoms of anxiety, it's much easier to address your distorted thought patterns and develop new feelings about yourself. Even when you can't control the anxiety-provoking situation, you'll know that you're still in control of yourself.

THE POWER OF RELAXATION

The first step in controling your physical and behavioral response to anxiety is learning to relax. The idea of relaxing seems deceptively simple, but it's actually a complex method for relieving stress, improving concentration, and increasing performance. When we reduce the amount of stress in our bodies, we become more alert, more aware, and more able to engage in any activity.

We think of relaxation as affecting our bodies, but it has an equally powerful effect on our minds. We're often aware of stiffness and tension in our bodies, but we rarely notice when thoughts are spinning through our heads, jumbled to the point of distraction. Relaxing the mind allows us to clear our thoughts and connect with what is actually happening and what we are actually feeling. Too often our anxiety is the product of what we think will happen and what we think we'll feel.

Relaxation slows down the physiological chain-reaction that causes the anxiety response. As our body relaxes, our brain receives the message that the fight or flight response is no longer necessary. The parasympathetic nervous system releases the neurotransmitter acetylcholine, which has the opposite effect of epinephrine and norepinephrine. When our body slows and relaxes, any unnecessary activity in the voluntary and involuntary muscles ceases.

It is possible to relax the muscles with tranquilizers, but this type of medication has a dulling effect on the brain. Tranquilizers may be prescribed by a physician for short-term treatment of an intense anxiety reaction, but depending on medication to deal with anxiety can actually make it worse.

Relaxing naturally through a systematic exercise program is a pleasurable process that can be used in any situation with immediate results. Natural relaxation works in conjunction with efforts to understand the deeper source of anxiety. Instead of clouding the brain, natural relaxation makes the brain more effective, so we can readily address the mental and emotional aspects of anxiety.

RELAXATION TECHNIQUES

Of the many relaxation techniques available, two work especially well to reduce mental and physical symptoms of anxiety. One is called *focused breathing,* the other is *progressive relaxation.*

Focusing on your breathing takes your mind off your symptoms, which keeps your anxiety from escalating. By remembering to take deep, regular breaths, you prevent the rapid, shallow breathing that can increase your physical discomfort. At the same time, the increased flow of oxygen through your bloodstream helps alleviate symptoms that are already present.

Allow yourself time to practice the relaxation exercises. You'll begin to recognize tension you weren't aware of, and you'll relax when the tension is released.

Focused Breathing

Focused breathing is an excellent technique to relax your mind and your body. Read through the exercise, then practice, following each step carefully.

1. Sit or lie down in a comfortable position in a place where you will not be interrupted for at least ten to fifteen minutes. Loosen any tight clothing: belts, ties, collars, shoes. If it makes you feel more relaxed, take off your glasses or contact lenses.

2. Begin by breathing out, letting go of the air that is now in your lungs. Pull in your chest and stomach to help push the air out.

3. Inhale slowly, mentally counting to eight. Count "one-and-two-and-three-and-four-and-five-and-six-and-seven-and-eight." Let your abdomen expand as you fill the lower part of your lungs, then fill your chest.

4. Hold your breath for another slow count to eight.

5. Gradually exhale, counting to eight one more time.

6. Repeat the exercise five times.

7. Breath normally for a minute, then repeat the cycle of five focused breaths.

8. As you get used to the exercise, try to complete five cycles of five focused breaths at each session, with a minute of normal breathing between each cycle.

Exhaling slowly is often the most difficult part of focused breathing. If you're used to blowing air out of your lungs in one puff, this slow exhalation process will be a challenge. Don't strain. If you only count to four before you feel the need to inhale, that's okay. As you accustom yourself to the exercise, you'll find that you can exhale more slowly. You'll soon be able to count all the way to eight before you need to take a breath.

If you have difficulty remembering how many breaths you've completed, use your fingers to count. On one hand, you can use one finger to count each breath as you complete it. On the other hand, count the completed cycles.

As you begin each cycle of inhaling and exhaling, try to relax the muscles in your shoulders, neck, and head.

Progressive Relaxation

Most people are not aware of the tension that exists in their bodies most of the time. This exercise helps you recognize when you're tense, so you can recognize the need to relax. Progressive relaxation is a technique that uses systematic tightening and holding of the body's muscles to increase relaxation. This technique can be used with focused breathing for an even greater effect.

As you work on the progressive relaxation exercise, notice how different each part of your body feels after you release the tension from it. First your right arm will feel different from your left. It may feel heavier, or it may feel as if it has more energy. After you release both arms, notice the difference between your arms and legs. At the end of the exercise, your whole body will be relaxed.

This exercise teaches you to tell the difference between tension and relaxation.

1. Sit or lie down in a comfortable position in a place where you will not be interrupted for at least ten to fifteen minutes. Loosen any tight clothing: belts, ties, collars, shoes. If it makes you feel more relaxed, take off your glasses or contact lenses.

2. Begin by inhaling, slowly.

3. Hold your breath and tighten the muscles in your right arm. Make a fist and feel the tension that develops in your hand, wrist, forearm, elbow, and upper arm.

4. When your entire arm is tense, release your breath and the muscles in your arm at the same time. Let your arm go limp.

5. Repeat the process with your left arm. Inhale, hold your breath as you tighten the muscles, then release.

6. Repeat the exercise for your right foot and leg, your left foot and leg, your abdomen, your chest, your back, your shoulders, your neck, your face.

7. Rest for a minute, breathing normally. Notice how the different parts of your body feel, and how your body feels as a whole.

If you initially have trouble relaxing with either the focused breathing or the progressive relaxation exercises, don't worry that you won't ever be able to relax. Think of the months and years that your body has been refining its anxiety reaction. You probably won't be able to relax completely in one day or even one week. But if you make relaxation a habit, you will eventually begin to feel the difference.

Like any skill, relaxation requires practice. Practice one or both exercises every day. Don't wait for a stressful event to trigger your anxiety. If you make relaxation part of your daily life, you'll be amazed by how quickly you'll conquer the physical symptoms of anxiety.

Resistance

Did you read through the two relaxation techniques without actually doing the exercises? Did you feel hesitant about making yourself relax? Maybe you imagine you wouldn't know what to do *without* your anxiety? Or maybe you're experiencing resistance.

Resistance is a psychological condition that keeps us from following through with our own best intentions. Whether we're resisting a prescribed treatment program or refusing to listen to a helpful suggestion from a friend, we're sabotaging our own process. But resistance is not simply refusal to change, nor is it stubborn behavior. Resistance occurs when elements in our unconscious minds prevent us from taking action.

The only way to deal with resistance is to bring our unconscious fears into consciousness. Dealing with our unconscious fears is even more difficult than learning to recognize our distorted thought processes. Our thoughts may have been negative and self-defeating, but they were very much part of our conscious thinking. We often have to dig for the hidden factors in resistance.

Resistance works like this. If you find yourself unable to even try the relaxation techniques your conscious mind might be thinking that reading them should be enough. But your *unconscious* mind is telling you that if you don't really try, you won't have to deal with failure when nothing happens. Better to blame the techniques, or yourself for being lazy, than to try and not succeed. Or, if you try some of the techniques, but don't practice them regularly: your conscious mind tells you the techniques don't work. You don't feel any more in control than when you started the book. Your unconscious mind might be working overtime, frightened by the possibility of success. What if the exercises do work? You might actually change. Then what would happen? There's a lot of insecurity and risk in change. What would you do without anxiety in your life? How could you cope with success?

Countering Resistance
The following technique will help overcome your resistance. You may be able to recognize the unconscious thoughts and feelings that keep you from progressing, or you may just move beyond them. Either way, you'll be able to take control of your anxiety.

Time Limits
1. Give yourself a limited period of time to follow the relaxation program. Before you actually begin, make an assessment of your levels of tension and anxiety. Then every day for one week, do the focused breathing and the progressive relaxation.
2. At the end of the week, evaluate your level of tension and anxiety.
3. If your tension and anxiety have decreased, allow yourself to continue the program for another week. Again, assess your improvement.

It's always difficult to make a life-long commitment. Knowing that we have a definite time limit helps us start any new course of action. Setting up a time frame also helps us evaluate our growth and improvement, because it's difficult to assess daily changes.

Accepting New Habits

1. Accept the fact that any program for change feels strange at first. Remember that you are trying to break habits and change behavior patterns that are almost as old as you are!

2. If you don't feel uncomfortable at first, try harder!

3. Remember that excitement feels a lot like anxiety. You may think you're going backwards just when you start to feel good about your progress.

4. Be prepared to feel good about your accomplishments. Allow yourself to accept any unfamiliar positive feelings, like elation, satisfaction, pride. You've earned these feelings! Enjoy them.

7 THE KEY TO EASE: REALITY

Not even the universe, with its countless billions of galaxies, represents greater wonder or complexity than the human brain. The human brain is a mirror to infinity. There is no limit to its range, scope, or capacity for creative growth.

NORMAN COUSINS
Head First

Imagine that you're to be in the spotlight to accept congratulations for an important achievement. Are you ready to receive praise graciously without being flustered? Or does the idea of getting any kind of attention start your mind racing with embarrassing possibilities? Do you mentally rehearse every blunder you could possibly make, anticipating public humiliation?

Or maybe your mind gets going *after* you've experienced a painful social event, replaying every anxious moment over and over, until you promise yourself, "never again." Despite all your efforts to overcome your social anxiety, do you feel frustrated, because you can't always shut out the negative images?

Perhaps you tried the relaxation exercises in the previous chapter, but found yourself interrupted by an anxious voice inside your head. Maybe the journal exercises have been helpful in theory, but when an encounter looms, you still feel waves of anxiety.

As bad as they may seem, all of these problems actually show something very positive about you. If you know how to use your mind to call up negative images about yourself, you're already familiar with the power of your imagination.

How often do the negative images you create come true? Maybe you foresee yourself having a miserable time at a party, but you force yourself to go, and indeed, you have a miserable time. Or you drive to a job interview, picturing yourself squirming over the difficult questions you're afraid you'll be asked. When the interviewer does ask the dreaded questions, you resign yourself to another failure.

Have you ever worked up your nerve to address a difficult problem at work, yet knowing full well that your colleagues will resent you? Under such circumstances, how can you feel good about proving yourself right?

What you might not realize is that with no more effort than you're already using to visualize failure, you can visualize success. Instead of setting yourself up for social misery, you can use your mental energy to imagine and achieve social ease.

THE POWER OF IMAGINATION

You use your imagination hundreds, probably thousands of times each day. When you open the left hand drawer of your desk to take out the scissors, you might not be aware that you pictured the scissors in that particular drawer before you acted. When you pull into a parking space, you probably don't realize that your mind sees the proper way to park before you do so.

Any athlete knows how important it is to focus the mind before a game or competition. The members of a team concentrate on their goal; any distraction can lead to poor execution. Breaking concentration is a sure way to lose.

Artists, designers, writers, and other people with creative jobs spend much of their day actively using their imaginations. Before a fifty-story structure can be built, it must be imagined by the architect, then visualized by the construction team.

Over the past several years, researchers in several fields have studied the effects of imagination on actual events. People involved with health-care, business, and sports have now documented what actors and actresses have always known: rehearsing a desired outcome enhances the actual performance.

We know that the ability to imagine, or visualize influences future results. But how do we learn to use our mental power to achieve positive, instead of negative results? And how can we tell if we're being positive or simply fooling ourselves?

CHANGING NEGATIVE THINKING

Social anxiety thrives on negative thinking. Each of the seven distorted thought patterns that were identified in chapter 2 is a different type of negative imaginative act. Whether you're generalizing, or using must/should, or win-or-lose thinking, your mental process is encouraging negative outcomes.

"So how do I learn to think positively?" you might ask.

It's important to realize that while positive is the opposite of negative, "positive thinking" is not the way to conquer social anxiety. Many popular methods of self-improvement blur the distinction between positive thinking and realistic thinking, which is unfortunate. Positive thinking, by itself, can be just as unrealistic as the distorted mental patterns we're trying to overcome.

WHAT IS REALISTIC THINKING?

Realistic thinking is based on an honest assessment of ourselves, the situations we're facing, and the people with whom we're interacting. We want to be positive and look for the best in life, but we need to keep our positive attitude in a realistic framework.

Realistic thinking is grounded in the objective world of verifiable facts, but it is also based on our inner truth. An unrealistically positive approach can lead us off-track, engaging us in a chase for impossible goals that will only increase our anxiety and diminish our self-esteem.

We know that predicting-the-future and mind-reading are unrealistic thought patterns, because in reality, we cannot know the future. When we foresee a worst-case scenario, our imagination is focusing on unrealistic, negative probabilities. But when we imagine a perfect outcome—the achievement of miraculous success—we're still deluding ourselves. We're still using unrealistic thinking, even though our minds are aimed in the positive direction.

Unrealistic, positive messages deny our true feelings as much as negative messages. Because our emotions are such a basic part of who we are, it's a struggle for us consciously and unconsciously, to believe something that feels wrong. So an unrealistic, positive message can actually hurt, by making us even more anxious.

Unrealistic Thinking: Janet

Janet's boss, the director of personnel, asked her to organize the annual Christmas party, starting with a speech to the entire company. This was a good opportunity for Janet, one that would give her exposure to top-level executives. But the idea of addressing one thousand fellow workers gave her a panic attack.

Janet's friend Howard suggested she think positively. He gave her some mental remedies to steel herself before the speech. Janet repeated what she hoped would be a confidence-building message to herself. "I am always perfectly calm," she said over and over. "My presentation will be perfect."

But the words didn't ring true. Inside, Janet was more worried than ever. On the day of the speech, she froze. She lost her concentration, and stumbled through her notes. She had no idea how the audience reacted; she was oblivious. All she could think about was what a mess she was making of her career. When it was over, she told her boss never to put her through such an ordeal again.

By creating a positive fantasy, Janet avoided the real issues, and put herself, unprepared, into a threatening situation. Instead of using the opportunity to overcome her fears so she could learn how to handle similar difficult situations, Janet allowed herself to be a victim of anxiety.

A realistic approach would have helped Janet realize that she had real feelings of anxiety about giving the presentation. By accepting her anxious feelings, she would have given herself the chance to explore her fears. Then she could have used her time to deal with them and to prepare her speech.

Having positive, but realistic expectations would have allowed Janet to understand that despite her nervousness, she was looking forward to speaking before her whole company. The presentation was a big step, but there was no reason for Janet to expect perfection of herself. Instead of expecting miracles and creating a disaster, Janet could have viewed the presentation as a first step and let herself enjoy the experience of learning.

Realistic thinking helps us manage ourselves. None of us can predict the future or control every outcome. Being positive in a realistic way means that we accept our weaknesses, and know that despite them, we can cope. We know that our self-esteem is not dependent on achieving any particular result. The ability to express our true selves, including our weaknesses, confirms a sense of personal value.

JOURNAL EXERCISE #1

The following exercise will help you distinguish between unrealistic and realistic thinking. Remember to be as specific as you can, and to look for any patterns in your responses.

    1. Think about a situation that is difficult for you.

    2. Think of a negative and unrealistic response to the situation. Then think of a positive, but still unrealistic response.

3. What distorted thought patterns influenced your responses?

4. Now think of a realistic, positive response.

5. List the advantages of your realistic approach.

If you're having difficulty getting started, read these excerpts from Janet's journal.

JANET'S JOURNAL

Situation: John, my boss, came in my office today and told me that the student intern project is behind schedule. We had proposed the idea of hiring students during the summer, and the company supported the concept. Now I've failed, because all the contracts aren't ready, so we can't follow through. He said that unless I get my act together, the whole department is going to look bad.

Unrealistic/ Negative Response: John is really angry with me. I don't blame him. He gave me an important job to handle on my own and I've shown that I can't be trusted with it. I'm a lousy person. I'll probably get fired before the year's out.

Distorted Thought Patterns: Mind-reading: He didn't say he was angry, and he didn't look angry. I shouldn't assume something unless he tells me.

Generalizing: Just because I haven't done such a great job on this project doesn't mean I'm a lousy person. Just because the project is late, doesn't mean the department will look bad.

Unrealistic/
Positive Response: I should thank John for pointing out this little problem. I should pull my act together immediately, because I must come through for my department. If I stay up every night this week, I'll be able to get the work in on time. John and the company will be so pleased they'll probably give me a big promotion.

Distorted
Thought Patterns: Should/Must Thinking: I'm saying that I have to be perfect and perform according to some ideal standard.

Twisted logic: I'm expecting a promotion and praise for doing work that I have to crank out in a state of panic. Mind-reading and predicting-the-future: I don't know how John will feel or how the project will turn out.

Realistic/
Positive Response: I appreciate John's warning. I realize now that it was a mistake not to let him know the problems I've been having. I admit that I felt inadequate, because it's taking me longer than he expected. It's up to me to let him know that I have been giving the project my best effort.

It's possible that he's not even aware of some of the problems, or that his expectations are unrealistic. I'm an intelligent person and good at my work. This is my first time on a big project like this, and it's natural to make mistakes. Next time, I'll be able to manage it better.

Advantages: It feels good to be honest about my mis-
givings, and it feels good to appreciate
myself and recognize my abilities. Rather
than expecting a specific outcome, either
good or bad, I can now look forward to
discussing the problem for what it is—a
difficult project, not a reflection on me.
This approach makes me feel good
about myself and my work.

As Janet learned, realistic thinking can be more positive than
positive thinking, because realistic thinking is based on trusting ourselves. As you complete the journal exercise, try to
focus on your feelings about yourself. Are you able to feel the
balance that realistic thinking brings?

CRITICISM AND COMPLIMENTS

When we're not secure in ourselves, criticism can be a sudden,
unexpected blow to our self-esteem. If we don't have a realistic
view of ourselves, it's difficult to separate ourselves from an
unrealistic appraisal. It's also difficult to recognize the value in
critical remarks.

Criticism: Robert

For the last year Robert has been working at becoming
more self-expressive. His efforts to get in touch with his
feelings and thoughts have greatly improved his self-
esteem. But the other night, while Robert was having
dinner with a close friend, he confided how pleased he
was with his personal growth. The friend, someone he'd
known since college, smiled and said sarcastically, "You
know what's wrong with you, Bob? You're perfect."

In reality, it is not possible to do anything, no matter how
small, and guarantee that you will please every other person on
the planet. As Robert found, even self-improvement can be
criticized.

But what was Robert's friend really saying? Perhaps he was agreeing with Robert, but expressing himself poorly. Or perhaps his response reflected jealously or his own feelings of inadequacy. Whatever his response meant, he felt close enough to Robert to make an effort to communicate with him.

In a very important way, criticism is actually a strong compliment. When someone cares enough to give criticism, they are acknowledging our existence. Like compliments, criticism indicates that some distinction is being made, that some aspect of our personality is being recognized. The only way to avoid criticism is to be a nonentity. Effective human beings have to accept that criticism is an unavoidable part of reality.

Bette Davis said, "Being seen as difficult is the beginning of success." Learning to feel comfortable with any kind of attention is an important part of overcoming social anxiety. Criticism puts us momentarily in the spotlight, just as compliments do. If we accept ourselves, we can appreciate both positive and negative feedback as part of the process of learning who we really are.

In *The Official Criticism Manual*, Dr. Deborah Bright, of Bright Enterprises, Inc., explains that criticism functions in our lives the same way that negative forces act in the natural world. Positive and negative elements create balance. Thinking of criticism as being either good or bad misses the point. Criticism is a source of knowledge. Criticism is the gift of knowing how we are perceived by others.

For many of us, *giving* criticism can seem much more difficult than accepting it. But if we perceive criticism realistically, we know that the opinions we give to others are no more absolute than the ones they give us. We can choose to accept their criticism or not, and they can accept or reject ours.

We would be irresponsible not to criticize when another person needs to be aware of our perceptions. Teachers learn to criticize in a positive way to help students improve. Supervisors are required to criticize the employees they manage, and if they resist problems may develop. Criticism given in an honest supportive atmosphere addresses minor problems while they're still minor and improves work relationships before they're impossibly damaged.

Criticism: Adelle

Adelle took her friend to a favorite restaurant, but was embarrassed by the poor quality of the food. Instead of saying anything to the waiter, Adelle apologized to her friend. She told herself that the waiter had nothing to do with the food preparation, and she didn't want to insult the restaurant owner by criticizing the food. She'd enjoyed many meals there, so she quietly paid the check and left.

But the incident left Adelle feeling unsatisfied and uncomfortable. Would the food be disappointing again? The next time she went out, Adelle decided to try a different place. When Adelle drove by her old favorite a few months later, she saw that the restaurant had closed.

Adelle's feedback might not have prevented the restaurant from going out of business, but it would have sent at least one message to the owners. Adelle could have expressed her opinion honestly. If she had said, "I've had many good meals here, but tonight my guest and I are both unhappy with the food," the owners may or may not have felt insulted, but either way, they would have gained a valuable insight.

The most common reason we avoid giving criticism is that we're afraid of the other person's reaction. But if we give criticism in a supportive way, the person's reaction is not a reflection on us.

If the restaurant owner had been insulted and rejected Adelle's comment, Adelle would have learned that the management was not interested in improvement. She would have had no qualms about spending her money elsewhere.

When we criticize and the other person reacts emotionally, we may feel that we caused their reaction. But just as we're not responsible for other's actions, we cannot control their reactions. Just as we can choose how to react to criticism, the people we criticize can choose their own reaction.

THE ART OF DESENSITIZATION

One way to become more comfortable giving and receiving criticism is to use our imagination to act out the situations beforehand. Instead of imagining a negative outcome, we can imagine a positive one, including new behavior and feelings that are realistic. By creating positive, realistic expectations, we desensitize ourselves to encounters that previously evoked distress.

Psychological desensitization is like the process people with allergies use to overcome their sensitivities. In allergy desensitization, patients are exposed to small amounts of the substance causing the reaction, until gradually, they no longer react at all.

In the same way, exposure to small, measured doses of anxiety allows our minds and bodies to adjust. Instead of responding automatically with anxiety, we gradually learn to react with less stress and more control.

The two basic techniques that we will use for desensitizing ourselves are called *visualization* and *mental rehearsal*. With the first, we use visual imagery to achieve relaxation and stress reduction. In mental rehearsals, we create entire scenes in our heads, imagining them as realistically as possible, so we can almost feel ourselves participating.

VISUALIZATION

Visualization allows us to create an image, a scene, or a situation in our minds. When we visualize an anxiety-provoking situation, our conscious mind learns how to respond to the situation, while our unconscious develops new physiological and emotional responses. Visualization lets us harness the powerful energy of our minds to overcome anxiety.

These desensitization exercises are preparation for real encounters. Once we've successfully visualized the situation, we can approach the real one confidently, knowing we'll respond, consciously and unconsciously, as we've rehearsed. As we become more comfortable with our mental rehearsals, we can begin to imagine more stressful circumstances.

A Special Sanctuary

Before we deal with anxiety-provoking situations, it's important to develop a positive, relaxing mental picture that we can call up whenever we need to, one that will combat our habitual negative thinking. We all have special images deep inside that symbolize comfort and safety. Visualizing this positive image creates sanctuary within us. Our special sanctuary becomes a powerful weapon against anxiety, one we can use whenever we feel the need.

VISUALIZATION EXERCISE #1

This exercise will help you gain a relaxed positive feeling about yourself, and will be the basis for future visualization exercises.

Read through the entire exercise before you begin. Try to remember the steps, so you won't have to break your concentration as you perform the exercise.

1. Sit or lie down in a comfortable position in a place where you will not be interrupted for at least ten to fifteen minutes. Loosen any tight clothing: belts, ties, collars, shoes. if it make you feel more relaxed, take off your glasses or contact lenses.

2. Take several slow, deep breaths. If you feel tense or nervous, you might want to begin with the focused breathing or the progressive relaxation exercises.

3. Close your eyes. Let your imagination create an image of a place that feels safe and comforting. Your image could be a place where you've actually been, or it could be somewhere you've only dreamed about. This is a place where you feel at peace with yourself.

Your image might be of a nest, high up in a tree, where the moon and stars pass overhead. Or you might imagine yourself walking on the sand, listening to the roar of the surf, watching the sunset paint the horizon. You might be on a mountain peak, or sitting beside a rippling brook. You might be running across a green meadow, surrounded by rolling hills. You might be curled up by a fire, with your favorite pet at your side.

4. When you have settled on your special sanctuary, create a detailed mental picture of the place. What does it look like? What do you hear? Are you lying down or moving around? How does your body feel? If your sanctuary has a special scent, what is it?

5. Now, let the image drift out of focus as you concentrate on your breathing for a minute. You can use the focused breathing exercise, if you like.

6. Call back your special sanctuary. Is it still vivid, or do you need to recreate it? If you do, mentally employ each of your senses, until your sanctuary seems real.

7. Now concentrate on your breathing again. After a minute, call your sanctuary back up. If necessary, focus the image until it is clear and vivid.

8. Alternate your concentration, first focusing on your special sanctuary, then on your breathing. Keep working until your image returns clearly and quickly when you call it to mind.

MENTAL REHEARSAL

Mental rehearsals allow us to address anxiety-provoking situations or people from a position of security. Because it's happening in our mind, we can control the situation, and we can control our response, over and over until we reach a state of relaxation.

To work successfully, mental rehearsals require realistic images. As our visualization skills increase, we'll learn to create very real scenes of confrontation in our heads. As our bodies adjust to a more relaxed, positive state, we'll move into more difficult mental exercises. When the time comes to handle real situations, we'll feel relaxed and confident.

MENTAL REHEARSAL EXERCISE #1

This exercise presents the basic format for rehearsing any situation that provokes anxiety.

To help you understand the technique, the exercise provides an example, but you can begin with any mildly uncomfortable situation, such as those you marked with a zero or a one on your Social Anxiety Inventory (chapter 1).

Read through the entire exercise and familiarize yourself with the steps. Practice substituting your own imaginary situation at the appropriate places.

Try not to break your concentration as you perform the exercise.

1. Sit or lie down in a comfortable position in a place where you will not be interrupted for at least ten to fifteen minutes. Loosen any tight clothing: belts, ties, collars, shoes. If it makes you feel more relaxed, take off your glasses or contact lenses.

2. Take several slow, deep breaths. If you feel tense or nervous, you might want to begin with the focused breathing or the progressive relaxation exercises.

3. Close your eyes. State the situation you're going to deal with today. For example, returning something to a store. Perhaps you bought a toaster last week, and it's already broken. Say aloud, "I am going to return the broken toaster to the store and get a new one."

4. Imagine each step you take toward your goal. For example, first, you pack the toaster into its box. You locate your receipt. You carry the box and receipt to the car. You drive to the store.

See yourself breathing slowly and evenly. Acknowledge that you are entitled to confront this problem. You arrive at the store and park your car. You enter the store and approach the counter where you purchased your toaster. If you feel any symptom of anxiety, recognize it, and focus on your breathing. Use focused breathing or progressive relaxation, until your breathing is once again slow and regular. You smile at the salesperson and ask for help. You explain the problem and show the salesperson your receipt.

Anytime your anxiety symptoms seem beyond control, call up your special sanctuary. Allow yourself to stay in this safe place until you feel back in control and your breathing is slow and regular.

As you wait for the salesperson to respond, you know that you will be able to handle whatever happens. The salesperson offers to refund your money or give you another toaster. You want a new toaster, but you ask the salesperson to test it first. The toaster works. You take it and walk out of the store.

You feel comfortable and relaxed. You feel good about your efforts and pleased with the results. You take the new toaster home, plug it in, and watch it work. You feel good about yourself, because you've just completed a difficult task.

5. Allow yourself a moment to feel proud of your accomplishment.

6. Now, let the exercise fade away, as you call to mind your special sanctuary. Allow yourself a minute to enjoy the peace you feel in your safe place.

7. Before you open your eyes, notice your breathing. Is it slow and even? Do your shoulders and neck feel relaxed?

8. Now open your eyes.

If you find it difficult to remember the steps of the exercise without breaking your concentration, you might want to make a tape recording that you can play as you create your mental rehearsals.

As you practice with the situations you've rated with a 1, you'll become familiar with the exercise format. When you reach a sense of comfort and security about handling your mild anxieties, you'll be ready to move on to a situation that provokes moderate anxiety, one of those you rated 2 on the Inventory. Eventually, you'll progress until you feel comfortable rehearsing the severe situations you marked with a 3.

MONITORING YOURSELF

After you begin to use the visualization exercises, you'll probably notice that you feel better about yourself. You might even feel good when you least expect to. Enjoy the feeling. You've done a lot of work to get where you are.

Don't be disappointed if you find yourself slipping back into negative thinking now and then. It's unrealistic to expect all your negative patterns to disappear so soon. And remember, the mind can be devious. Your subconscious will likely catch you off-guard with *new* negative tactics.

A sabotage frequently employed by the subconscious is acceptance of the "wise saying" that actually twists important lessons you've already learned. You might be surprised at the number of maxims and adages that foster distorted thought patterns. If you find yourself "preparing for the worst," stop and do a reality check to make certain you're not predicting-the-future by assuming the worst.

You might find yourself thinking you are doomed to fail because "history repeats itself" or "once a loser, always a loser." If you're confused about what is realistic and what is not, think the situation over carefully.

It may help to go back to Journal Exercise #1 on page 143 and write down as many different views of the situation as you can. Writing down your unrealistic/negative or unrealistic/positive reactions to any experience will help you discern what is realistic and positive for you.

PRACTICING VISUALIZATION

If you still find it difficult to call up mental images effectively, you can practice with some basic visualization exercises. Sit comfortably, as you do in the regular exercises. Relax and close your eyes.

Mental Imaging Practice #1

1. Picture a square. Picture a circle. Picture a triangle.

2. Repeat three times.

3. Now, picture a square, then turn it so it becomes a diamond. Picture a circle, then turn it into a sphere. Picture a triangle, and turn it upside down.

4. Picture the square, then turn it into a circle, then turn the circle into a triangle.

Mental Imaging Practice #2

1. Picture someone you know very well, for example, your mother.

2. How is your mother dressed? What is she doing? Where is she going? Is she alone? How will she get to her destination?

After you complete the practice exercises, call up your special sanctuary. Is the image clear? Can you feel it with all of your senses?

Notice how your body feels. Is there any tension, or are you relaxed and comfortable? Appreciate yourself for the effort you are making, then open your eyes.

YOUR SOCIAL ANXIETY PROFILE

By this time, you're aware of the different types of people and situations that provoke your anxiety. You've also learned how to identify the facets of your appearance, background, and social skills about which you feel self-conscious.

But are you aware of the progress you've made so far? Your journal exercises and the relaxation and visualization exercises probably already have had an impact on your symptoms of anxiety.

This would be a good time to go back over the Social

Anxiety Inventory in chapter 1 and the Social Anxiety Feelings Inventory in chapter 2. Depending on the amount of work you've been doing, you might also review the inventories in chapters 5 and 6.

As you review the inventories, feel free to make changes. Your level of anxiety may have decreased, but if instead it has *increased*, don't feel that you're regressing. You're probably just more aware of your true feelings than you were when you first completed the inventories.

JOURNAL EXERCISE #2

This exercise will help you prepare a Personal Anxiety Profile, using the information in your inventories. Feel free to add any new information you've gleaned from your journal exercises.

Remember to be as specific as you can and to look for any patterns in your responses.

YOUR PERSONAL ANXIETY PROFILE

1. Using any or all of the inventories, make a list of the anxiety-related issues on which you'd like to work.
2. Using the Social Anxiety Inventory in chapter 1, make a list of the people or types of people around whom you feel most anxious. Be as detailed as possible.

   For example, do you feel anxious around: your mother, your father, a particular friend, friends in general, your neighbors, your boss, other authority figures, men, women, strangers, younger people, older people? Organize your list from least to most anxiety-provoking.
3. Now look at your Social Anxiety Feelings Inventory in chapter 2. The inventory is divided into three categories, so you can identify the feelings you have around: (1) Professional acquaintances; (2) Family, friends, and people with whom you are intimate; (3) strangers or people you scarcely know.

Do any of the three categories show more feelings rated 2 or 3 than the others?

Make a list of the particular social situations that seem to stir the most anxiety. Be as specific as possible: going to casual lunches, attending formal meetings, giving a report, being the center of attention, hosting a party. You might look at the Social Anxiety Inventory, chapter 1, for some clues. Organize your list from least to most anxiety provoking.

4. Using your Generic Anxiety Inventory in chapter 5, make a list of any personal quality or characteristic with which you're uncomfortable. Look for the questions you rated 0 or 1, but include others if they seem important. Organize your list from least to most anxiety-provoking.

The four lists you have made are your Personal Anxiety Profile. The lists will help as you work to desensitize yourself to anxiety.

PROGRESSIVE DESENSITIZATION

The desensitizing program is similar to the mental rehearsal exercise you've already learned. Once you've reached a level of comfort using mental rehearsals, you're ready to create your own desensitization program, using your Personal Anxiety Profile as a guide.

From your Profile lists select a situation, person, or element about yourself that you want to work on. It's best to ease into the program by starting with items at the tops of your Personal Anxiety Profile lists, the ones that cause the least amount of anxiety for you.

The desensitization exercise involves three stages: *relaxing*, *rehearsing*, and *relearning*. It's important to be fully relaxed before you begin. When you're relaxed, you'll visualize an imaginary scene that includes the elements you selected from your Profile. You'll rehearse the scene mentally, until you feel at ease. Once you're able to handle the scene comfortably in your mind, you'll recreate the scene in reality.

It's important for you to monitor your progress at each stage of the exercise. Be completely comfortable before you move on to the next stage.

It's also important that you be comfortable with each exercise before you move to the next one. Begin by tackling one mildly difficult element at a time. Then you can move to a more difficult situation, or you can combine several mild elements into one exercise. Your goal is to plan your desensitization program, so you can move from the least anxiety-provoking elements to the greater anxiety-provoking ones, achieving a feeling of ease at each level, before you move on to the next.

DESENSITIZATION EXERCISE #1

Review your Personal Anxiety Profile lists. Select the situation, person, or element about yourself that you want to work on. You may combine items from two or more lists. For example, you can create a scene that combines an uncomfortable situation with something uncomfortable about yourself. Or you could think of a person that you feel anxious around in an uncomfortable situation.

It may help you to combine elements, or it may make the exercise more difficult. If you combine elements and can't overcome your anxiety, go back and work with one item at a time. After you feel completely comfortable, you can try combining the elements again.

RELAXING

1. Sit or lie down in a comfortable position in a place where you will not be interrupted for at least ten to fifteen minutes. Loosen any tight clothing: belts, ties, collars, shoes. If it makes you feel more relaxed, take off your glasses or contact lenses.

2. Take several slow, deep breaths. If you feel tense or nervous, you might want to begin with focused breathing or progressive relaxation exercises.

3. Close your eyes. Now, call to mind your special sanctuary. Allow yourself a minute to enjoy the peace you feel in your own safe place.

REHEARSING

This stage of the exercise should immediately follow the relaxing stage.

4. With your eyes closed, state aloud the scene you're going to create today. What is your goal?

5. Imagine each step you make in achieving your goal.

6. Feel yourself breathing slowly and evenly. Approve of yourself for confronting this difficult matter. How do you feel? Is your body relaxed? Do you feel good about your efforts and pleased with the results?

7. When you've accomplished your goal, let the exercise fade away. Now, call to mind your special sanctuary. Allow yourself a minute to enjoy the peace and safety you feel in your own safe place.

8. Before you open your eyes, notice your breathing. Is it slow and even? Does your body feel relaxed?

9. Now open your eyes.

10. If you don't feel that you achieved a total state of ease, plan to repeat the same scene for your next exercise. You may want to increase your exercise time to fifteen to twenty minutes, to give yourself long enough to visualize the entire scene and be comfortable.

Special Notes For Beginning Desensitization

- If you feel any symptom of anxiety, recognize it, and focus on your breathing. Use focused beating or progressive relaxation, until your breathing is once again slow and regular.

- If any symptom feels out of control, call up your special sanctuary. Allow yourself to exist in you own safe place until you feel relaxed again, and your breathing is slow and regular.
- After you feel relaxed, try to call up the scene again. If you still feel symptoms of anxiety, tell yourself that it's good that you're in touch with your true feelings. Let the scene fade, and call up your special sanctuary.
- If any scene creates feelings of anxiety that you can't resolve by repeating the relaxing stage of the exercise, you need to simplify the scene. Eliminate an element, if you've combined more than one. Or go back to a less anxiety-provoking element from your Profile lists.

When you feel completely at ease with the scene you've just rehearsed, you're ready to move on to the relearning state, where you recreate the scene in real life.

CREATING SCENES IN REALITY

Some of the situations on your Profile will be fairly simple to recreate, like being honest with a friend or criticizing someone at work. These scenes are part of your everyday world.

Other scenes will require you to invent ways to get the right person or type of person into the particular situation you want to confront. Some of the more difficult exercises will work better if you arrange for progressive steps that take you toward your overall goal. Each step then becomes a separate relearning exercise that you'll want to accomplish with ease before moving on to the next.

It might help to see how other people have structured their reality to fit their personal needs. In the two examples that follow, Carol and Robert devised small steps to allow themselves to gradually adapt and adjust, rather than tackling their complex situations as one huge exercise.

Carol's Relearning Exercise

Carol was the young reporter we discussed in chapter 1 whose first attempt to speak in public ended in what she considered a personal disaster. But Carol worked very seriously on her anxiety problems, and eventually became comfortable addressing large groups.

Relearning: Carol

Carol felt her first speaking engagement was a failure. Nevertheless, she was asked to speak again, this time to a group of reporters. Before she accepted, Carol made sure that she would have plenty of time to research and write her speech. Her anxiety about her ability to inform and entertain an audience was one of the areas she wanted to focus on.

With the speech still two weeks away, Carol arranged for a friend to listen to the draft she'd prepared. She made notes about her friend's reactions to the information in the speech, and to the bits of humor she added. She revised the speech until it felt right.

Then she practiced giving the speech, allowing herself to deal with the generic anxiety she felt standing before an audience.

First, she visited the hotel ballroom where she would be addressing the reporters. Then, in her own house, Carol practiced reading the speech in front of a mirror. Next, she invited several friends over and read the speech to them, while she imagined herself standing in the ballroom.

By the night of her second speech, Carol felt fairly comfortable both with her speech and with giving it in front of others. She still had some anxiety about being the focus of attention, but she did her best to accept her feelings.

While Carol was being introduced to the audience, she chose not to listen. Instead, she concentrated on her breathing. She called up her special sanctuary image, and allowed herself to feel at peace for a moment.

The speech was a definite success. Carol allowed herself to feel good about her efforts. The next day, she made a list of the many ways she had improved since her first speaking engagement. She also made a list of the specific feelings of anxiety she had experienced, so she could develop new exercises to continue working on them.

Robert's Relearning Exercise

After Robert's divorce, he developed feelings of anxiety about dating. The first year, he managed to stay at work late almost every night. On weekends he stayed home, visited his family, or spent his time with necessary projects and errands. With the encouragement of a friend, Robert began to recognize that he was avoiding dating because of anxiety.

After competing the inventories, working in his journal, and making a Personal Profile, Robert decided to relearn the process of dating.

Relearning: Robert

First, Robert agreed to meet a blind date for dinner at his friend's house. After rehearsing the dinner party mentally, he approached the actual event with some excitement.

Robert and his date knew most of the people at the dinner party, so he felt safe and comfortable. He could talk to his date, and they could listen to and observe each other without feeling the need to perform or win approval.

The next step for Robert was arranging an evening out with two women in his office. They agreed to meet at a nice restaurant, so he got the chance to practice dining out, but he didn't have to deal with the preliminary rituals of picking up a date, and he didn't feel responsible for all the conversation. By going out with women he knew, Robert was able to experience women as friends again, something he'd almost forgotten. He remembered that spending time with women could be enjoyable.

For his next step, Robert decided to ask out a woman

friend from his married years. Going out with someone he already knew helped him feel safe and comfortable. He knew the woman was attractive, but she looked even better than he'd remembered. Robert felt pleased that he had a date with someone so appealing.

The Relearning exercises gave Robert the confidence to meet more people and allowed him to take the time to enjoy himself. He eventually organized a video dating service, because he found that, after his own experiences with anxiety, he could offer people some good advice about feeling comfortable, even on a first date.

RELEARNING

This is the third stage of the desensitization exercise. When you're ready to recreate your scene in real life, go back and repeat the relaxing and rehearsing stages, imagining your scene until it's comfortable. Then bring your scent to life, following these steps.

1. Take several slow, deep breaths. If you feel tense or nervous, you might want to give yourself time to use focused breathing or progressive relaxation exercises.

2. Call to mind your special sanctuary. Allow yourself a minute to enjoy the peace you feel in your own safe place.

3. As you begin to experience the scene in your life, see yourself breathing slowly and evenly. Acknowledge how far you have come. You have the right to confront this problem, regardless of the results. You are doing this for yourself, because you respect yourself.

4. During the actual encounter, think about how you feel. Allow yourself to feel comfortable and relaxed. You have every reason to feel good about your efforts. If you recognize any symptoms of anxiety, concentrate on your breathing. If you need to, call up your special sanctuary. If neither of those help, simply withdraw.

5. When the actual experience comes to a close, allow yourself a moment to feel proud of your accomplishment. Whatever happened, you have every reason to feel good about yourself, because you've just dealt with your anxiety in the most real way.

6. If possible, call to mind your special sanctuary. Allow yourself a minute to enjoy the peace you feel in your own safe place.

7. Now, notice your breathing. Is it slow and even? Does your body feel relaxed?

Some Notes About Relearning

- Just as in the rehearsing stage, you'll want to monitor your feelings and symptoms of anxiety. If you feel that any symptom is beyond your control, allow yourself to withdraw.
- If you're trying to talk to someone, simply excuse yourself and go to a safe place. If the location is part of the problem, simply leave.
- Withdrawal is not a sign of defeat, but a way to increase your control over yourself. You are in charge of this program. It's up to you to determine when you're ready and for what.
- Before you approach the actual scene again, rehearse it once more. Pay careful attention to the symptoms you felt in the real situation. Can you determine the source of your anxiety?

JOURNAL EXERCISE #3

This exercise will remind you of the many positive things you can learn from even the most miserable experiences. You will be able to loosen the strings that tie you to your past, and at the same time, appreciate yourself more.

1. Write a description of a real-life experience that was particularly traumatic or embarrassing. Some examples:

killing an animal, even accidentally; being homesick when you went away to camp; being rejected by a club or team; an awkward sexual encounter; a disappointing relationship; a job you messed up; a promotion you didn't get.

2. Allow yourself to recall the feelings you felt during the actual experience. Write down how you felt, and any negative thoughts that strike you. How did this experience hurt you as a person? What effect did it have on your life?

3. Now, rewrite the experience as a piece of fiction. Take full poetic license, changing any detail, including the outcome. The only requirement is that you turn the experience into a positive event.

4. When you've completed your fictionalized view of your experience, reread the original description. How do you feel about the real experience now?

5. Make a list of what you learned and what you gained by having gone through the real experience. In what positive ways is your life different because of it?

8 AT EASE WITH INTIMACY

We are not all equally vulnerable to the anxieties of court-ship, but we are all vulnerable to some extent. Finding someone to love who loves us in return is at the core of human happiness. Courtship is a primary path toward this love. When the goal is so crucial and the process seems so mysterious, how can we help but feel anxious?

DR. JUDITH SILLS
A Fine Romance

Everyone needs emotional and physical intimacy; both are basic components of health and happiness. But how do you satisfy this need when meeting people and getting to know them causes you severe anxiety?

You could avoid the problem entirely and resign yourself to living alone forever, but are you really willing to take such a drastic step? You could ask your friends to accompany you on social occasions and depend solely on friendships to fill your need for intimacy, but no matter how good such friendships are, they can rarely fill our deepest needs to love and be loved.

There is an alternative. What if you could learn to accept your anxiety about meeting new people and risking intimacy. What if you actually could learn to enjoy getting to know another person through dating? The good news is, you *can*.

WHY IS DATING SO DIFFICULT?

Dating is different from other relationships. In business relationships, we connect with other people because they share our goals and interests. When we make friends, we recognize in other people qualities we share and admire. Mutual recognition grows gradually into a friendship. But from the time we're adolescents, before we ever go on our first date, we have specific expectations about what dating should and should not be.

We don't spend our time fantasizing about the kinds of friends or business associates we want; we meet people, realize we enjoy spending time together, and develop a relationship. But when people are potential dates, the rules change. We scrutinize them, examine their possible opinions of us, predict the most likely outcome of our first meeting—all before we even get to know them!

Finding a partner to love is a basic human need; it would be unhealthy to ignore our yearnings. Whether we just want someone special to have fun with or whether we're hoping to develop a long-term relationship, what we really need is someone to whom we can open ourselves, someone who will know, accept, and love our true inner self.

It's not surprising that the prospect of finding just the right person fills us with anxiety. Although love is a basic need, our methods for finding it have evolved into a complex, unnatural process. If only we could approach dating in the same way we make friends! Instead of being traumatic, dating could be one of the most enriching and pleasurable parts of our lives. In opening ourselves to others, we have new chances to discover aspects of ourselves we might otherwise never have known.

Intimacy: John
John is from the Midwest. He attended college, earned a degree in political science, and returned to his small hometown to work in the local bank. Although John spent time with girls in college and considered several of them

to be friends, he never asked any of them for a date. John is now twenty-nine, and he knows most of the single young women in his area. But he's convinced that if he asked one out, the whole town would be talking about it. And besides, none of the women he knows are "right for me, anyway."

Intimacy: Suzanne

Suzanne, an attractive thirty-seven-year-old, has been divorced for two years, but as yet hasn't started dating again. Suzanne's ex-husband was violent and domineering, and Suzanne is afraid that any man she meets could turn out the same, a monster in disguise.

Intimacy: Kimberly

Kimberly is forty-three. She lives in a large city, and although she has a lot of friends, both male and female, Kimberly doesn't know anyone she considers a potential mate. Kimberly joined a computer dating service, hoping to find Mr. Right, but even though she's dated several men, none of her dates have led to a serious relationship. When her friends ask why, Kimberly explains that she likes going to shows, concerts, and fancy restaurants, and none of the men she's met are really her type.

Intimacy: Michael

Michael just turned forty-eight, and he admits to being a workaholic. He hasn't lost touch with his group of friends, but only sees them when he finds himself free and they're available. Michael hasn't given up on the idea of finding someone to share his life, but he knows that the kind of women he'd like to date would never put up with his crazy, frantic schedule. After all, that was what killed his last relationship.

We all know people like John, Suzanne, Kimberly, and Michael. None of these people think of themselves as having social anxiety; in fact, they are not even aware that anxiety about intimacy is the reason they avoid relationships. Instead of accepting themselves and learning to deal with their feelings, they've created elaborate protection systems, not realizing that their defenses are obstacles to happiness.

John has never been able to admit, even to himself, that he knows very little about women. Although he had female friends in college, the friendships were more a matter of hanging out with a group of people, some of them women. John has never had an intimate relationship with a woman, nor has he really known a woman as a close friend. Instead of facing his inexperience and trying to do something about it, John uses the narrow-mindedness of his small town as an excuse to avoid dating.

When he assumes that the whole town would be talking if he were to start dating someone, John is predicting-the-future. Because he isn't really acquainted with any of the women in his town, he can't *know* that none of them are right for him. He's mind-reading. By focusing on the results he has predicted instead of getting to know women, John is shutting himself off from the true pleasure of dating.

Suzanne is also stuck in distorted thinking. Her ex-husband, who was sweet and considerate during their courtship, turned into a monster, so Suzanne generalizes that the same thing would happen again.

Suzanne is still dwelling-in-the-past. What if another man turned out like her husband? And what if she were too blind to see it happening?

Instead of giving herself credit for learning from the past and getting out of a bad situation, Suzanne is allowing her fears to control her. She is protecting herself, but she's also holding herself back from a second chance at happiness. It is probable that she will make more mistakes in her life, but it is realistic to think that she won't make the same mistake twice.

Kimberly is a victim of unrealistic expectations. She doesn't consider any of her male friends to be perfectly suited to her ideal of a future mate. Even though Kimberly meets new men and enjoys their company, they don't come up to her preconceived standard. If she were honest with her dates about her feelings, they probably wouldn't ask her out again, so Kimberly must always hide her true self. Her unrealistic outlook prevents Kimberly from enjoying the present and makes true intimacy impossible.

Michael has developed a work compulsion to hide the anxiety he feels about potential dates, about himself, and about the future. He is generalizing and dwelling-in-the-past, assuming that because his last relationship broke up over his work, so would any future relationship.

Michael uses mind-reading to preclude his chances of finding a new relationship. By insisting that anyone he might like wouldn't put up with his schedule, Michael sounds like the old Groucho Marx joke: "I wouldn't want to be in a club that would want me for a member!" Michael avoids facing the reasons for his behavior, but he might wake up in ten years and wonder what happened to his chances.

A DATE ANXIETY INVENTORY

You may not know your thoughts, feelings, and perceptions about dating as well as you think you do. Making an inventory can help you discover the specific sources of your dating anxiety.

Respond to the following questions as honestly as you can. If a question deals with a situation you've never experienced, visualize yourself in that experience, and imagine how you would respond.

It might help you to remember a recent experience with dating anxiety before you answer the questions. Try to recall as many specific feelings, fears, and doubts as you can. The Dating Anxiety Inventory can make good use of those potent negative reactions.

YOUR DATING ANXIETY INVENTORY

Rating Scale: Let your answers reflect your thoughts and feelings, as well as your experiences.

0 = Rarely, or never
1 = Sometimes
2 = Often
3 = Always

Do you worry about if:

The person you want to go out with will call you?	0	1	2	3
The person you want to go out with doesn't call, should you just wait?	0	1	2	3
The amount of money you make will matter to the person you want to date?	0	1	2	3
The person you want to date might not approve of your career?	0	1	2	3
You'll ever find an ideal mate?	0	1	2	3
The perfect sexual partner exists?	0	1	2	3
Your next date, even if it should develop into a relationship, will end like all the others have?	0	1	2	3

Your past relationships
have failed because of
something that's wrong
with you?   0   1   2   3

Do You Wish:

You could find some-
one who could change
the negative pattern in
your life?   0   1   2   3

That Prince Charming
and Cinderella weren't
just fairy tale characters?   0   1   2   3

*Before You Go Out
With Someone For The
First Time Do You:*

Worry if your date will
find you attractive?   0   1   2   3

Worry if you will find
your date attractive?   0   1   2   3

Decide what to wear,
then change your mind
several times, and fi-
nally run out and buy
something new?   0   1   2   3

Worry about what
your date will be
wearing?   0   1   2   3

Worry that your date
will want to have sex
before you want to?   0   1   2   3

Worry that your date
won't want to have sex
when you do?   0   1   2   3

Worry that you won't have a good time, and plan how to tell your date you don't want to go out again?	0	1	2	3
Worry that you'll want to go out again, but your date won't want to?	0	1	2	3
Worry that if this date turns out badly, you won't ever want to go out with anyone again?	0	1	2	3
Rehearse the evening, so you can please your date in every way?	0	1	2	3
Hope that this date might be the person that will solve everything?	0	1	2	3
Ever think about calling up and cancelling your date at the last minute?	0	1	2	3

EVALUATING YOUR INVENTORY

If you've answered 2 or 3 to most of these questions about dating, you're aware of your true feelings, thoughts, and perceptions, even though they may be uncomfortable to think about. If you feel anxiety about dating, but your responses are mostly 0s and 1s, you might be under the influence of the myths and faulty thinking that fuel your dating anxieties.

THE MYTH OF PERFECTION

Several of the questions on the dating anxiety inventory concern perfection. Is there an ideal mate? Does the perfect sexual partner exist? Even worrying about the way we look, or how our date will look, or what we should wear are expressions of perfection anxiety.

The concept of perfection is one of the most dangerous and destructive myths in the human psyche, because it inflicts us with impossible and wasteful yearnings. Perfection doesn't exist, and every person in the world has a different concept of what perfection is, or would be, if it did exist.

When we wish for perfection, we are forever removing ourselves from the present. We can never be truly alive in the moment. Looking for perfection means never seeing reality.

By searching for the perfect mate, we overlook a lot of people because they don't match our ideal. Part of the fun of dating is exploring ourselves and other people. In the process of getting to know other people, we often learn and expand our horizons. If our minds are made up before we start, we shut ourselves off from millions of possibilities. The very concept of perfection means there is no need to grow or change.

The myth of perfection is destructive in other ways, too. When we strive to meet someone else's idea of perfection, we give ourselves away. The cliche of the "perfect little wife" grew out of the terrible reality that many women subjugated their own needs and desires to fit the ideals of their husbands. Even if your perfect person existed, would you want to spend the rest of their life with a prefabricated ideal, instead of an independent, interesting, growing person?

It is normal and healthy to want someone to share our life with, someone to experience fulfilling sexuality with, someone to rely on, and someone who will rely on us. All these goals are realistic, if we're willing to work at them. Love is not a static state, but a process that requires constant work from two people who are committed to their relationship.

It's natural to be on our best behavior when we're dating.

It's natural to want to make a good impression, because dating is the process of being open to possibilities for the future. But an honest relationship cannot develop unless we are willing and able to show our real selves.

"What if I'm a slob?" "What if I can't dance?" "What if I really like to stay home and watch old movies?"

It might be scary at first, letting another person see the real you, but think of how good it will feel when you can relax and enjoy *yourself*. And think how fulfilling it will be when you find someone who falls in love with the real you.

THE MYTH OF THE PERFECT DATE

The myth of perfection can turn our best-laid plans to shambles.

The Perfect Date: George

George designed the perfect date for Betsy, a woman he met through work. He bought flowers, picked her up in a limousine, took her to one of the most expensive restaurants in town, then to a nightclub for dancing. He was totally stunned when Betsy refused to go out with him again.

George's elaborate, expensive date was like the prize awarded on The Dating Game. So, what went wrong?

Betsy, the woman George took on his perfect date, was someone he had just met, someone he barely knew. What did their first date accomplish? Betsy got to know George's idea of a good time, but did he get to know hers? Did they get to know each other better?

No, George admits, they didn't really have much of a chance to talk. The only thing he learned was that she was a good dancer.

George couldn't help being disappointed. Even though he'd given the date considerable thought and spent a lot of money trying to impress Betsy, she responded in the worst way possible. Despite all his plans, George hadn't really given himself a chance.

Just as every person has a different idea of perfection, we each have our own idea of what would make the perfect date. While one person would love a sailboat ride under a full moon, another person would get seasick at the thought. Most of the time, a perfect evening is something that just happens spontaneously when two people feel good about themselves and about each other.

Maybe Betsy thought she'd be spending a quiet evening getting to know George better. Perhaps she felt George was being an extravagant showoff. George will probably never find out exactly what went wrong. But all his efforts weren't completely wasted, because he learned an important lesson.

A few months later, George met a woman named Annette. He wanted to ask Annette on a date, but wishing to avoid another fiasco, he just said, "So, Annette, what kind of things do you like to do when you're not working?"

"Concerts," Annette said. "And ballet, I love the ballet."

George smiled politely, but shook his head and admitted that he didn't really like that kind of stuff.

"Ice-skating," Annette suggested. "Have you ever been ice-skating?"

George laughed. "I haven't been ice-skating since I was a kid!"

"Me either! Annette said. "And I was never very good. Did you learn how to skate backwards?"

"Sure," George told her. He wasn't lying; he'd actually been a good skater when he was younger. "I bet I can teach you. Want to go?"

"Sure," Annette smiled.

George's date with Annette cost him a lot less money, and it turned out to be a lot more fun that his perfect date. George and Annette had fun skating, and they had time to talk when they stopped for hot cocoa later. George learned that he could be himself, really get to know another person, and still have a good time.

OUR SECRET FEARS

As if it weren't bad enough that our brains are filled with distorted thoughts and myths, we have another frailty: fear. When the subject is dating, we're battling four basic fears: fear of failure, fear of rejection, fear of our sexuality, and fear of the future.

Fear of Failure
The quest for perfection derives from our basic fear of failure. When we compulsively orchestrate every detail of living, we are fighting, not facing, our fear of failure. We have the erroneous belief that if we do everything exactly right, we can't fail, and we'll win undying love and approval.

But when we stop and think about it, we realize that there is no absolute right any more than there is an absolute perfection. We all have our own idea of what is right, and if we're open and flexible, our concept of what is right is fluid and changing.

Real life doesn't conform to our transitory ideas of what is right, or what *should* be. In real life the wine cork gets stuck in the bottle and the theatre tickets get left at home. We pick a nice restaurant for a special occasion, only to find out that the food is lousy. We get dressed up for a party, and find out that everyone else is wearing casual clothes. By attempting to have everything exactly right all the time, we only set ourselves up for frustration and failure.

When we learn to accept ourselves as we are, with all our imperfections, we no longer have to fear failure every minute of the day. We no longer feel that life's normal flow of good and bad is a personal attack, meant to diminish us. Instead, we learn to deal with problems objectively. And most important, we can share our true selves with others.

Fear of Failure: Alan

Alan is an average-looking thirty-two-year-old who works as a computer programmer. Alan has an unspoken, but conscious rule about dating. He will only go out with gorgeous women, and his idea of beauty matches the one sold by Playboy Magazine. Most of the women Alan asks out reject his offers, and he rarely takes anyone out more than once. At some point in Alan's life, he made the absolute assumption that women who are beautiful are perfect. He has convinced himself that he must have his idea of the perfect woman or no one at all.

Alan's generalization is a modern version of the myth of Pygmalion—the sculptor who hated women for their imperfections. Pygmalion refused to marry. Instead, he created his concept of perfection, the most beautiful sculpture ever created, a life-like stone carving of a woman. Then, unable to help himself, Pygmalion fell madly in love with his ideal.

Alan's search for perfect beauty may have developed from an insecurity about himself. He may be trying to compensate for something he feels is lacking in himself, either physical beauty or some other characteristic that he feels the perfect woman can provide.

If Alan could just learn to look at himself more realistically, he would discover many good qualities that balance what he feels are his flaws. Only when Alan learns to accept himself will he be able to relate to a woman as a human being, instead of an icon.

Fear of Rejection

If you answered 2 or 3 to any of the first four questions on the Dating Anxiety Inventory, you are experiencing the fear of rejection. The fear of rejection is so much a part of dating that it's difficult to draw the line between normal concern and anxiety.

It's normal to feel curious, excited, nervous, and even worried when we're facing a new situation. It's healthy for us to feel a rush of emotions when we're contemplating a potential for pleasure and fulfillment. But anxiety about asking someone out on a date can be more than just a natural reaction to dealing with the unknown.

Fear of Rejection: Fred
Fred met someone he really liked at his AA meeting. He got the woman's phone number from a mutual friend, but then he couldn't bring himself to call her. He spent several evenings trying to call, practicing what he would say, making notes in anticipation of what she might say. But he never made the call. He decided that she probably wouldn't remember him, so why bother?

Fear of Rejection: Jacqueline
Jacqueline met a nice man one night at business school. She hoped he'd ask her out, but when he didn't, she decided she would call him. He sounded surprised to hear from her, but accepted the date. On the day they were supposed to go out, Jacqueline called him and cancelled. She told him an emergency had come up at work, but she told herself it was better not to go on the date, since she already knew how it would turn out.

For Fred, the idea of asking for a date provoked much more than a healthy amount of tension. By generalizing, Fred came to the global conclusion that this one phone call would determine his future—at least his future with this particular woman. Fred scarcely knew the woman, so realistically he couldn't know if he would want to have more than one date with her, even if she agreed to go out the first time.

Fred was also mind-reading. Instead of making the call and asking the woman if she remembered him, he assumed she wouldn't. Or he assumed that if she did remember him, she wasn't favorably impressed. Even if that were true, which Fred had no way of knowing, asking her out on a date might have changed her mind. The way for Fred to find out was to make the call, but instead he fell prey to negative thinking and fears.

Fear of rejection and fear of the unknown work hand in hand. If Fred's worst assumptions were right, if the woman really didn't want to go out with him, his effort would end in rejection. But if she accepted and they went out, then he'd have to deal with an even larger arena of unknowns.

What if she actually liked Fred? Or what if Fred felt disappointed and didn't want to go out with her again? How would he tell her? Or would he just avoid her? What if they had a good time on the first date, but then she didn't want to go out with him again? Whether any of these threatening possibilities were conscious or not, they may still have influenced Fred's decision.

By falling into the pattern of predicting-the-future, Fred was really saying that he should be perfect and never make a mistake. Fred wasn't satisfied living his life: he wanted to predict what would happen in it with absolute certainty.

Jacqueline managed to overcome her fears of immediate rejection. She called the man she wanted to know, but then she became the victim of distorted thinking—dwelling-in-the-past and predicting-the-future. In the last two years, Jacqueline had gone out with several men, but none for more than a few dates. Each man seemed to have a good time with her, until he got to know the details of her work. At least, that's the mind-reading assumption she made.

Although Jacqueline was attending business school at night to complete her degree, she worked as an analyst for a large financial services company. Whenever she felt good about someone, just when it seemed that a relationship could develop, she let her guard down and her success, or salary, or independence always seemed to turn him off.

We've all had bad experiences, and we all know the feeling of not wanting to repeat them. If we learn from our mistakes, we can allow ourselves to have positive expectations for our future. But if we feel that a past mistake was our fault, that it was caused by something inherently wrong with us, then our future takes on a bleak aspect.

Instead of looking at her past relationships in an objective way, jacqueline blamed herself. She was efficient, organized, quick-thinking person, but she had come to perceive herself as a strong-willed businesswoman who overpowered men.

If Jacqueline had let herself be open from the beginning, she probably would have saved herself a lot of grief. Before going out on an actual date, she could have spent time casually with a man she liked, and let him know about her life, including the benefits and limitations of her position. By assuming the worst about all men, Jacqueline cut herself off from plenty of them who might have been thrilled to meet her. Although she was trying to protect herself from more pain, her secretive behavior actually created a pattern of continued rejections.

No one likes to be told no, but what's important is what that no means to our sense of identity. Many of our deep psychological needs may be revealed to us when we are rejected. To be truly healthy, we need to become aware of these needs, so we can meet them realistically.

After Jacqueline spent some time understanding what rejection meant to her sense of identity and self-esteem, she realized that she had many good points. No matter what anyone else thought, she loved her work, and she appreciated the qualities that made her good at her job. She also realized that she wouldn't be happy with a man who was unable to accept her efficiency and directness—not to mention her salary.

When Jacqueline began to understand and accept her true self, she no longer felt the need to hide. She soon noticed that the men who started asking her out were also successful in their work.

Fear of Sexuality
Fear of our own sexuality is really another aspect of the fear of intimacy, of revealing our truest self to another person and to ourselves. The fear of sexuality is very different from the fear of rejection. We want to protect ourselves from rejection, but we want to achieve a relationship that includes sexuality.

In any new relationship, the question of when to become sexually involved usually occupies a lot of our time. The answer is simple. If two people know each other and trust each other enough to feel comfortable revealing their inner selves, then sexual communication can be a positive form of self-expression.

Whether sexual intimacy develops during courtship or after marriage, it still involves revealing our most vulnerable selves to another person. In addition to concern about our physical desirability, we all feel curiosity and a certain amount of anxiety about our sexual compatibility with our partner. Wanting to find someone to develop a good sexual relationship with is a normal human desire, but expecting to find the perfect sexual partner is unrealistic.

In a culture based on instant gratification, we regularly hear of sexual incompatibility as an excuse for a failed relationship. But by applying realistic thinking to sexual expectations, the twisted logic behind this concept becomes apparent. If no two people are alike, how could two people be alike sexually? And why would having the same sexual style be better than having different styles?

Like every other human characteristic, our sexuality is unique to us. Part of the pleasure of developing a sexual relationship comes from learning about our sexual responses and those of our partner. Part of the pleasure of marriage, or a committed, long-term relationship, is having plenty of time to learn and explore.

Sexual incompatibility occurs when two people aren't communicating. Both partners might be willing to overlook other communication difficulties but when they can't communicate sexually, they have to admit their problem.

Whenever we feel insecure, vulnerable, or pressured to have sex, or if we doubt our own or our partner's sincerity, then sexuality becomes difficult. The fear of being asked to be sexual when we're not ready can bring out a rash of anxieties.

Because sexuality involves all our emotions and all our senses, sexual communication is a profound way of expressing the feelings we have about ourselves and our partner. Sexual communication requires the same acceptance of ourselves as other forms of self-expressive communication. When we're neither honest about nor accepting of our feelings, the close-ness that sex requires can be frightening.

Fear of The Future

The future is the storehouse of our hopes and dreams and goals. Sometimes anxiety about dating awakens unsettled questions about ourselves. Sometimes when we start to care about someone and get involved with that person's life, we are forced to confront parts of ourselves that we've managed to avoid.

Fear of the Future: Sally

Sally, thirty-nine, is a nurse who's attending night school for a degree in public health. Sally started dating Wally four months ago. They get along well and see each other at least twice each week. Now that they've become sex-ually intimate, Sally finds herself feeling anxious before Wally comes over. She knows that if they have sex, he'll want to spend the night, and although she enjoys their time together, she likes being able to start her day by herself.

Although her sexual relationship with Wally brought out Sally's feeling of anxiety, sex wasn't the real problem. When Sally finally told Wally her feelings, they were able to have an honest discussion that helped them both understand what was happening.

In many ways, Sally and Wally felt good about their new relationship. What they discovered by sharing their feelings and thoughts was that they each had a different vision of the future. Wally hoped that their relationship would continue and that they would eventually be married. Sally didn't want a long-term relationship. She had a lot of career goals she wanted to meet before she started thinking about getting married.

By facing her anxiety, Sally realized that she was playing dangerous games with her emotions and Wally's, letting herself become totally involved, then trying to tell herself she wasn't. She also learned that Wally's ideas about marriage were very different from her own. She had always believed that getting married meant giving up her independence and her career.

Wally was well aware that Sally was committed to her work, and he had no intention of asking her to give up her goals. Sally realized that it wasn't marriage she was afraid of, but losing her dreams of the future.

Instead of causing a break-up, Sally and Wally's discussion brought them closer together. After a lot of thought, they decided to try living together. Sally felt nervous about making an open-ended commitment, so they agreed to try the arrangement for six months.

They both felt that they needed several months to adjust themselves to the kind of openness and intimacy that living with another person involved. At first it was difficult for Sally, to find a balance between being open with Wally and wanting her own private time and space. But once she learned to express her needs, they developed a gratifying relationship.

What If I Don't Want a Long-Term Relationship?

Sometimes we want to date because it's fun to spend time with another person in a personal way, but we don't want to find a life-long partner. There is nothing wrong with dating for fun, as long as both people are clear about their intentions. There's no reason we can't go to a movie, or try out a new restaurant, or go to a party with someone we like, without making a commitment to the future.

But it's important to ask ourselves if we're being honest. It's easy to avoid loneliness when someone offers companionship. How many of us have accepted dates with people who cared about us, when we knew we couldn't return the feeling? How many of us were honest enough to admit that we were using another human being in a way we would hate to be used?

To really enjoy dating, whether on a casual or serious basis, we have to be able to communicate openly and honestly.

Asserting our thoughts and feelings can be difficult, especially when we care about someone and don't want to hurt them. But hiding our feelings is not only dishonest, it's also destructive.

In addition to hurting someone else, our emotional evasiveness hurts us, creating a layer of self-deception between our conscious self and our feelings. We usually don't realize that when we lie to another person we're also lying to ourselves. Any act of dishonesty is an affront to our self-esteem.

The next time you ask someone out or accept a date just for fun, ask yourself some questions. Does the other person know how you feel about them and about your relationship with them? Do *you* know how you feel?

If you can talk honestly and comfortably about the relationship, then you'll both feel at ease, no matter what you do together.

DATING VISUALIZATION EXERCISE

Imagining the worst is one of the ways we make ourselves anxious about dating. Instead of wasting our imaginative powers on ideas of failure and rejection, we can use our minds constructively by creating positive images that will help ease our anxiety.

1. Sit or lie down in a comfortable position, somewhere you won't be interrupted for fifteen to twenty minutes.

2. Let yourself relax. If necessary, practice a relaxation technique—focused breathing or progressive relaxation.

3. Now picture yourself in the situation you are concerned about; for example, asking someone out. If you want to ask someone out, imagine the two of you standing together in a familiar place. Picture yourself as being calm and relaxed, and the other person as being very comfortable. Imagine yourself saying to the other person, "Would you like to go out with me?" Practice the words until they feel very comfortable.

Remember, you can't control the other person's response; that would be an unrealistic expectation. But you can imagine yourself feeling comfortable whether the person answers yes or no. Even if the person turns you down, you can feel good about making the effort.

If, on the other hand, you are anticipating a date that you've already made, imagine yourself preparing for the date. You feel calm and relaxed as you pick out your clothes and get dressed for the evening. You are looking forward to the evening, not worrying about it, as you go to meet your date. Your breathing is deep and even. Your voice is calm as you greet your date.

If you're going out for dinner, imagine the restaurant. Visualize yourself walking with your date to your table and sitting down. See yourself talking comfortably together. Your posture is relaxed and natural. Having dinner with this person feels completely natural. You enjoy talking with each other during the meal. You make eye contact. You feel at ease.

4. Bring the exercise to a close by imagining your special sanctuary. The comfort of your own safe place will reinforce the peaceful feelings you have attained in your visualization exercise.

Remember that your visualization exercise is a form of rehearsal. By giving yourself a positive, yet realistic, practice session, you will be able to relax and enjoy the actual experience.

JOURNAL EXERCISE #1

This exercise will help you bring yourself into focus, so you can see yourself from a realistic, positive perspective. Being able to appreciate your positive qualities will help you share yourself with other people.

1. Make a list of your qualities, attributes, positive values, and achievements. Don't think about dating or what might please anyone else. Just write down anything and everything that makes you feel good about yourself.

2. Go back to your list in a week and add any other positive aspects of yourself.

Robin, a salesperson for a large computer hardware company, made the following list for herself.

ROBIN'S GOOD QUALITIES

1. I get along well with the people I work with.
2. I am compassionate. I really care how other people feel.
3. I was the top salesperson in my department.
4. I helped raise my younger brother and sister.
5. I like kids.
6. Kids like me.
7. I taught myself to play the flute.
8. I know how to save money.
9. I can make a great meatloaf.
10. I've read lots of good books.

Look back over your list whenever you feel the need to remind yourself of your good qualities. Remember that these qualities are permanent aspects of you. Whether a particular date turns out the way you hope it will or not, you will never lose all the wonderful qualities that make you a valuable individual!

JOURNAL EXERCISE #2

Now comes the difficult task of facing the less-than-perfect parts of yourself. Awareness of your weak spots will help you remember that, like everyone else, you're not perfect. Accepting your frailties will help you interact with other people.

1. Make a list of your shortcomings. Remember that these are elements of yourself that you feel could be improved. Don't put down complaints from other people. This is your personal gripe list.

2. Respond to each of your shortcomings with a realistic analysis of how that problem affects your life.

3. Do any of your problems jeopardize your dating aspirations? If so, what could you do to change?

Gary, a librarian at a university, made this list.

NO, I'M NOT PERFECT

1. I can't dance, never could.
2. I don't have much money, and I'm a bit stingy.
3. When I see a beautiful woman, I get tongue-tied.
4. I hate to write letters, even though I like people to write me.
5. I don't know anything about cars, or engines, or anything mechanical. And I'm not the least bit interested, either.
6. I wish I made more money, but I don't do anything about it. (Lazy???)
7. I like to sleep late.
8. I hate cleaning my apartment.

Here are Gary's realistic responses to his problems.

1. So I don't dance. Why do I have to go out with someone who dances? There must be other people in the world who don't dance. To tell the truth, the dancing scene bores me.
2. Money is a problem for me, but not all women expect a man to pay for everything. I wouldn't feel good about someone who did. I like to have fun, but I have to be careful. Some women might respect that.
3. I'm insecure about my looks, so I think a beautiful woman would make fun of me. But that's really mind-reading. Besides, beauty isn't the only quality that matters.
4. I better not date by correspondence.
5. So what? Lots of people don't know anything about cars. That doesn't make me useless. I know lots of other things. I tend to mind-read and generalize when I assume that all women want a guy who's good with cars and motors. Maybe I can meet a woman who can check the oil and change a tire.
6. I need to work on some job possibilities, so I can make more money. I don't like feeling stingy, but as it is now, I have to protect myself. I wouldn't want to depend on someone else's money, so that is a definite area I should work on.

7. I've been telling myself I'm lazy, but maybe I sleep late because I'm not happy with my job or my financial situation. Maybe if I felt better about my future, I wouldn't want to sleep so much.

8. I don't think I'll ever learn to enjoy cleaning. But maybe I'll end up in a relationship with someone who likes to clean, and I can take over a chore that she hates.

Our flaws make us human; as long as we're alive, we can improve. Looking at our shortcomings with a realistic attitude puts them in perspective and helps us disassociate our weaknesses from our dating anxiety.

When you are able to accept yourself—shortcomings included—then you can believe that other people will accept you. If getting specific about your problems motivates you to improve, then you know you're changing because you want to, not because someone else says you should.

ANALYZING DATING SITUATIONS

You may be aware that you have dating anxiety, but do you know exactly what dating situations make you most uncomfortable? You might feel relaxed when you go out to a movie or a casual dinner, but just dreaming about an exotic date makes you anxious. How would you really feel if you got a chance to do something you've always wanted to do on a date?

JOURNAL EXERCISE #3

Getting specific about dating situations will help you see more clearly where your anxieties are centered.

1. Make a list of every kind of date and dating situation you can imagine. Include all the situations you've ever dreamed of experiencing—and don't avoid situations that give you anxiety just thinking about them! Here are some examples:

going to a fancy party
going to a football game
going to a movie
going out with someone you don't know
going out with someone as a favor for a friend
going out with someone you admire very much
going away for a ski weekend
going to the tropics for a week
going bowling
going to the beach
going birdwatching
going on a picnic

2. Now, go back and rate each situation for the amount of anxiety you feel thinking about it, using a 1 for slight feelings of anxiety, a 2 for noticeable feelings of discomfort, and a 3 for severe feelings of anxiety.

3. Rewrite your list, so that all the situations you rate with a 1 come first, then all the 2s, then any you rated 3. Remember that situations rated 1 and even some rated 2 reflect fairly normal feelings about dating.

4. Using the Dating Visualization Exercise, practice the situations on your list, beginning with those rated 2. Gradually, over several days or weeks, you'll feel comfortable enough to move on to the 3s.

5. As you complete each visualization exercise, make notes in your journal about any thoughts or feelings you had while you were imagining yourself in a particular situation. Keep a record of your insights. You can go back and read it when the time comes to practice the situation in real life.

DATING DESENSITIZATION

You can reduce your anxiety about dating by creating situations that will allow you to practice each type of date step by step. When you begin, you might be able to accomplish some steps by yourself. Then you might ask a friend to stand in for your date. When you're comfortable with the practice step, then you can progress to the real thing.

Use your ranked list of Dating Activities. Begin with a situation that responded well to the visualization exercise.

1. Begin with one of your Dating Situations that you rated as a 2, and practice the situation as though it were real. For example, if one of your situations is calling someone you barely know for a date:

pick up the phone and pretend to dial;

ask for that person;

imagine that person on the other end of the phone as you speak out loud, asking for a specific date;

imagine how the person answers;

then respond, out loud.

How do you feel? Did the practice make you feel anxious? Keep practicing until it feels easy.

2. Continue practicing, moving through your list from the lower anxiety situations to higher. Don't move on until you feel completely comfortable with each situation.

3. Monitor your symptoms of anxiety as you practice each situation. If any symptom increases, practice the relaxation techniques. Say to yourself as you inhale: "Anxiety is a habit." Then exhale and say to yourself: "I can break this habit, because I want to."

THE MESSAGE OF ANXIETY

We talked earlier about social anxiety bringing you a message about something of which you were previously unaware. Anxiety about dating carries the same type of message. If you feel anxiety in any dating situation, stop and become aware of your thoughts. Try to complete this sentence in your head, until you run out of ideas: I feel anxious because _____.

If possible, make notes so you can review the ideas you came up with.

The message anxiety brings is always important, but sometimes it brings a serious warning. Overcoming anxiety means paying attention to it. Anxiety-provoking situations need to be dealt with, not avoided.

What if you were on a date, and your date got drunk and wanted to drive? Your anxiety in such a situation could save your life. What if you went out for the first time with someone you didn't know, and you discovered that the person was dangerous?

When we accept ourselves as we are, we make it possible to learn from the message anxiety brings, whether it's positive or negative. Paying attention to anxiety can improve our lives.

TEN TIPS FOR DATING EASE

1. *Relax.* Practice the relaxation techniques before tackling any situation that might cause anxiety. Physical relaxation will lower your level of emotional anxiety. If you feel relaxed, so will the people around you.

2. *Assert yourself.* Nothing increases anxiety like losing control. Practice the self-assertive communication exercises in chapter 4. Take responsibility for your feelings, and don't accept responsibility for anyone else's.

3. *Know yourself.* Learn your good qualities and your shortcomings. Spend time thinking about who you are now and who you want to be in the future. How do you like to spend your time? The more you know about yourself, the more comfortable you can be setting up dating situations that feel good.

4. *Be realistic.* Think positively, but don't get stuck with unrealistic expectations. You can't control what another person does or thinks; spend your energy taking care of yourself. Evaluate your goals honestly, and don't create impossible, perfectionist obstacles to happiness. Getting to know another person takes time. Don't expect instant fireworks on your first date.

5. *Use realistic thinking.* It's easy to get stuck in the patterns of distorted thinking, but perhaps the worst is predicting-the-future. When you assume the worst will happen, you usually end up avoiding a situation, ask yourself *why*. Counter any distorted thoughts with realistic responses.

6. *Be flexible.* Don't expect the world to adjust to your standard. Every social group has its own particular social rules, and learning how other people do things can be fun and enlightening.

7. *Be practical.* Most dating anxiety can be relieved if you evaluate a dating situation from a pragmatic standpoint. If you're going out with someone you don't know, why spend an evening together? Why not meet for coffee and see if you hit it off? If you're driving someplace with a new friend, you might investigate transportation alternatives in case you decide to come home early. If you're in a city, take cab fare.

8. *Use humor.* When we learn to accept ourselves and not expect perfection, it's easy to see the humor in some of our anxious situations. Woody Allen has built a career by making fun of himself as an anxiety-ridden New Yorker, yet he always comes off as loveable. You might try to diffuse a tense situation by asking if your date is as nervous as you are. Then you can compare the ridiculous thoughts and mishaps you've had and see whose are worse.

9. *Accept yourself.* In many cultures, surrender is held to be a source of great strength and wisdom. Surrender in this sense means accepting yourself. If you can learn to accept your anxiety, and to accept the imperfections in yourself and in your date, you will gain a sense of power.

10. *Focus yourself.* Don't focus on your anxiety or your problems, but on your purpose. The purpose of dating is to get to know another person. Look at the person you're with, listen to them. Watch how they treat you, how they treat others, how they handle different situations.

By paying attention to reality, you can really get to

know someone, not your idea of who they should be. Imagine you are a detective or an investigative reporter, and it's your job to find out what makes your date tick.

When you get to know another person, something amazing happens. The stranger becomes a friend, some-one you know and trust. As your positive feelings grow, your anxiety diminishes, and you feel more at ease.

9 SOCIAL EASE

"The cocktail party . . . is a device either for getting rid of social obligations hurriedly en masse, or for making overtures towards more serious social relationships, as in the etiquette of whoring."

BROOKS ATKINSON

*F*amily get-togethers, weddings, dinners, birthdays— whatever the occasion, parties are part of life. Ideally, parties are affirmations or celebrations of the joy we take in living. As human beings, we feel a need to connect with each other to reaffirm our relationships and to share significant events with people who are important in our lives.

But for many of us, parties are far from enjoyable. The idea of either attending or hosting a party throws us into the clutches of anxiety. Sometimes, we're not aware of the reasons for our discomfort, but even when we do recognize the pangs as social anxiety, most of us consider such feelings unacceptable.

If we don't want to participate in life's celebrations, we feel that something must be wrong with us. So we usually force ourselves to participate, despite our fears. Only rarely do we accept our feelings and take the time to examine their roots.

Parties are complex situations that bring together many sources of social anxiety. Accepting our feelings of anxiety makes it possible to analyze the party situation realistically.

For all of us, parties involve both known and unknown elements. Even a formal affair can't be completely planned or rehearsed. Many parties are spontaneous and unstructured happenings, which is part of the reason they're fun. But we have to feel self-confident to allow ourselves to participate and go with the flow.

Parties by their nature force us to deal with many people. There will be people we know, and usually, there will be some people we don't know. Some of the people we know will be people we want to see, so the party presents a pleasant opportunity to meet in a comfortable spot and talk.

But the same party can also precipitate a tense situation or an unavoidable confrontation. There might be people present who we know and *don't* want to see! And there might also be some people we'd like to meet—which triggers a different kind of tension, including feelings of generic anxiety.

Parties can evoke every aspect of generic anxiety—especially anxiety about appearance—but also anxiety about background, education, and social status. As if that weren't enough, attending a party can stimulate one or all of the four big fears: fear of rejection, fear of failure, fear of sexuality, and fear of the future.

When we are not accepting of ourselves, parties can seem like trials of our worth. But the opposite is also true. When we approve of ourselves, parties can be joyous occasions that give us validation. If we're unable to assert ourselves, we can easily feel intimidated by others. But when we feel comfortable expressing ourselves, talking with other people is a way to grow.

ACCEPTING OUR FEELINGS

Now, let's imagine a party and see if we can pinpoint some of the emotions and behavior that make parties feel like such traumatic events.

An Imaginary Party

It's Saturday evening, and you're getting ready for a party. You've been anticipating the event for weeks, planning exactly what you're going to wear. But when you get dressed, nothing seems to fit right. You hate the way you look so you throw your clothes off and rip through your closet, trying to find something else. Nothing works! Finally, you try on your last hope. It's not great, but it will have to do, unless you decide to give up and stay home.

You're not only disappointed about your clothes, you're angry at yourself. Just as with so many things in your life, you never seem to be in control. If it were earlier in the day, you'd call up and say you can't come, but they're expecting you to bring the dessert. You spent all afternoon making your special chocolate cheesecake.

So, you tell yourself not to think about how you look. You take the cheesecake, which looks great, and you're on your way. You try not to be nervous as you ring the doorbell.

Someone you don't know opens the door and shows you in. You clutch your cheesecake tightly, grateful that it gives you a purpose for being there. You head for the kitchen, smiling politely, but not stopping to talk to any of the familiar faces in the crowded room.

To your dismay, the kitchen counter is filled with delicious-looking cakes and cookies. You look at your precious cheesecake and worry that it won't make the grade. Maybe you should just wrap it up and sneak out with it. You could go back home and eat the whole thing by yourself. Just then, your host Jan sees you.

Jan is not only the host of the party, but also your supervisor at work. You feel like saying something about all the time you spent on the cheesecake, but you decide to keep your mouth shut. Jan absent-mindedly takes your cheesecake out to the buffet. She asks what you'd like to drink, and looks surprised when you say, "Soda, please." "Great," you think, "now she thinks I can't handle alcohol." Jan puts the glass of soda in your hand and disappears.

You look around the room. You recognize about half the faces—all people from work. But even though you've been at the company for a year now, you don't know any of these people well.

You see Tom, standing to the side of a loud group. Tom seems to be having a great time, listening intently, smiling and laughing. You don't feel like barging in on their crowd, so you head back into the kitchen.

Barry has center stage in the kitchen. He's entertaining two women you don't recognize with witty remarks. You watch as he acts out little scenes that seem to delight his listeners. None of them notice you, so you leave.

Back in the dining room, Lois leans against a wall, watching. She's just the way she is at work, distant and aloof, and a little superior. You watch as she leans over the buffet to pick out a canape. As you look her way, she seems to smile slightly, but she makes no effort to speak, not even to say hello.

On the patio, Lisa and Daniel are engaged in a spirited discussion. They both smile and wave, but go on with their conversation.

You've made the rounds, and it looks as though it's going to be a dismal night. Maybe if you'd been able to wear the clothes you'd planned on, you'd feel more comfortable, and people would be a little more open. Starting up conversations is not one of your strong points. Everyone seems to be having a good time but you.

You try to calculate how long you'll have to stay so you don't appear impolite. Next time, you tell yourself, you'll know better.

ANXIETY DISGUISES

We've all experienced disappointment and anxiety in situations like this, but how many of us know that our negative reactions are the result of unrealistic expectations and inaccurate evaluations? Let's take another look at the typical nerve-wracking party and see what's going on beneath the surface.

Preparation Anxiety

The myth of perfection gives rise to false expectations. Before the party even starts, you're set up for an unrealistic outcome. You expect yourself not only to look nice, but to look *great*. Anything less is unacceptable and inadequate.

In reality, there is no such thing as a perfect look, unless, of course, you're modeling for a magazine advertisement and have hours of help from make-up artists and lighting experts. Whenever you feel you must appear perfect, you're removing yourself from the reality of the moment.

When we try to attain perfection, we're hiding our true self behind an acceptable veneer. It's impossible to find a style or a response that will please everyone. And spending our energy trying to please others prevents us from finding out what pleases us.

Taking a realistic approach to party-going doesn't mean that we should ignore details such as what we'll wear. Whether formal or informal, parties are special occasions, and dressing up can be part of the fun. But a realistic preparation focuses on feeling good about ourselves and being able to enjoy the party, not on presenting a flawless facade.

As soon as you feel anxious about not looking right, you can fall into a cycle of ever-increasing anxiety symptoms. Disappointment and anger lead to avoidance, which you counter with you must/you should thinking. Telling yourself that you *have* to attend a social function denies your freedom of choice. When your freedom is denied, you feel trapped, which makes you more anxious than you were to begin with.

It would be within your rights as an individual to call at the last moment and explain that you can't come to the party. In reality, your attendance at a social event is seldom required, even though other people may expect you to be there. It's important to remember that you're not responsible for what other people think; you're only responsible for yourself.

When you accept your freedom to choose, you can feel good about a decision to attend, even if the party doesn't turn out as you expected. But creating a false reason for going to the party—such as using your wonderful cheesecake as an excuse—denies your true feelings about attending the party and seeing other people. When you realize later that your cheesecake isn't even needed, you only feel more anxiety because you placed so much importance on it.

Making An Entrance

By focusing on how important your cheesecake was, you missed your initial opportunity to greet people. It's often easier to get involved with a peripheral issue, because it helps you avoid facing your anxiety. But then you have to pay the cost of ignoring your anxiety, which is missing the real purpose of the party: the chance to see and talk with other people. (When we host a party, it's this same type of anxiety that causes us to pay more attention to the food and drinks than to our guests. When the party is over, after all the time and effort we've put into it, all we can say is, "I hardly got to talk to anyone." We feel like we missed it, because we did miss what the party was really about.)

Your hostess, Jan, seemed very preoccupied. While you were feeling somewhat anxious about attending the boss's party, she was probably feeling anxious about entertaining the whole department. She certainly didn't seem to notice your effort on the cheesecake, which truly deserved some attention. There's no reason you couldn't have reminded her, saying, "It's my favorite recipe. Hope it's good!"

Despite Jan's lack of attention, there was no reason for you to feel unsure of yourself and begin mind-reading, just because you asked for a nonalcoholic drink. What to eat and drink at parties, whether to eat or drink at parties, how much to eat or drink—these are the subject of countless books on social etiquette. The answer is really simple: Why not enjoy ourselves?

Food and drink can be a problem for those of us who must follow special diets. Explaining the situation to our host ahead of time removes the anxiety from the actual event.

The choice to drink alcohol is a personal one. Unless we

drink too much, there is no reason to be concerned with other people's opinions. If we feel pressured to drink, we need to assert ourselves. What someone else thinks is not our responsibility. It is not our role in life to live up to other people's ideals, but to find our own.

Conversation Anxiety

You've barely arrived at the party and already you've had to face a barrage of anxiety-provoking incidents. Now it's time to deal with the ultimate in party tension—talking with the other guests.

Although it appears that all the people at the party are enjoying themselves, a close look will usually prove that the reality is different from the appearance. Let's begin by looking closely at Tom—your friend from work who's standing near a group of people, smiling and laughing.

Did you notice that Tom is not really involved in the group's conversation? He's standing near other people who are talking, he's listening to them, and he's smiling and laughing along with them, but he's not talking to anyone in particular. He probably doesn't feel comfortable enough to get involved in the conversation, so he only pretends to be involved. Tom may not even be aware of his own behavior. In addition to fooling others at the party, he might be fooling himself.

Let's go into the kitchen, where Barry was entertaining the ladies. Barry seems to be the perfect party guest, but is he really at ease, or is he simply trying to hide his own anxiety? Many people over-compensate by talking all the time, so they don't have to recognize their own anxious feelings. They dominate conversations, until other people get tired of listening and drift away.

Most people want conversation to be a two-way street. True conversations are not planned performances, but giving and sharing communications that reveal our inner selves. When people like Barry can't control the conversation, their anxiety returns, so they hurry off to look for another audience to entertain.

Hiding Anxiety with Compulsions

Let's look carefully at some of the other people at the party. What particular mannerisms are people using that might actually be ways to disguise nervous behavior?

One of the most common hiding techniques is compulsive eating or drinking. With a full mouth, anyone has a good excuse to avoid conversations.

You notice Lois standing near the buffet. Lois always apprears superior and aloof, and you automatically assumed that she perferred standing alone, exercising her judgment over the appetizers. But there's a real possibility that Lois is hiding her anxiety, avoiding other people, and taking refuge in the chips and dip.

There's nothing wrong with using the party snacks as a way to meet other people. The food table is a natural place to run into people who aren't already involved with others. And reactions to the food might be an interesting conversation starter. But spending the evening at the punch bowl can also be a way to avoid the fear of rejection or the fear of intimacy.

Another clue to understanding Lois is her aloof behavior. Standing apart from others is another way to avoid the responsibility for starting conversations. When we see ourselves as better, or different, from others, we excuse ourselves from the need to be initimate or sharing.

Avoiding People

You ran into two people on the patio who seemed to be enjoying themselves. But in fact, Lisa and Daniel spent the entire evening talking to each other, even though they see each other at work every day. Their behavior is another way of avoiding the party. Instead of taking chances and trying to connect with people they don't know well, they hide out and hold back from the evening's opportunities.

EXAMINING OUR OWN AVOIDANCE BEHAVIOR

The extreme of refusing an invitation is in many ways more honest than the indirect behaviors we adopt to avoid anxiety provoked by parties and social functions. Do any of these avoidance behaviors sound familiar?

Last minute change of plans. Do you have a knack for coming down with a cold just before a party or social engagement? Or is it your car that always seems to cause you unexpected trouble? Maybe you can't go to one party because you have another commitment—although you suspect that the first engagement might be cancelled and when it is, you're too late to make it to the other party.

Good reasons for not going. Do you ever find yourself lying or making up excuses so you won't have to attend parties or special events? Do you spend a considerable amount of time and energy figuring out how to avoid situations that sound like they might be uncomfortable?

Work comes first. Do you ever find yourself working late when you're supposed to be at a friend's party? Workaholics are often hermits in disguise, using their jobs as excuses to avoid social intimacy. If you have an office in your home, beware! Artists, computer whizzes, and others who work at home often become unaccustomed to social interactions and find it easier to stay at home than to get dressed up and put on a party hat.

MANAGING PARTY ANXIETY

Whenever we consciously shun meeting other people, whether for an ordinary lunch or a huge high school reunion, we limit our potential as human beings. The decision not to attend a party might be truly unavoidable, but it might also be the first step on a path of social isolation.

Social isolation is almost always caused by poor self-esteem. When we accept ourselves and learn to see the world realistically, we no longer need to escape from those who are open to our friendship.

JOURNAL EXERCISE #1

Rating your reactions to different types of parties will help you plan a program for managing anxiety.

 1. Make a list of every kind of party situation you've ever experienced, including any you might encounter some-day. Don't forget to list party situations that give you anx-iety just thinking about them! Here are some examples.
- formal event
- semi-formal high-school reunion
- college reunion football game
- holiday office party
- New Year's Eve dance party
- pool and yard party
- wedding shower with games
- wedding reception
- surprise birthday party for a friend
- surprise birthday party for you
- sit-down dinner with your in-laws
- buffet dinner with your spouse's colleagues
- trendy party with important people

2. Now, go back and rate each situation for the amount of anxiety you feel thinking about it, using a 1 for slight feel-ings of anxiety, a 2 for noticeable feelings of discomfort, and a 3 for severe feelings of anxiety.

3. Rewrite your list, so that all the situations you rate 1 come first, then all the 2s, then any you rated 3.

4. Begin with the party situations you rated with a 1, and write a description of what you would expect to encoun-ter. When you finish the 1s, write descriptions for the 2s, and 3s.

5. After waiting at least a day, reread your descriptions. Can you see any signs of unrealistic expectations? Write these down.

USING VISUALIZATION

Now that you know your expectations about the types of party situations that create anxiety for you, you can use the basic visualization exercise to mentally rehearse the situations on your list. Begin with those rated 1, and allow yourself to feel comfortable before moving on to the situations rated 2. Gradually, over several days or weeks, you'll feel comfortable enough to move on to the 3s.

Be sure to begin each visualization exercise with focused breathing or progressive relaxation. Call up your special sanctuary at the beginning and end of each exercise, so you can learn to associate the peace and relaxation you feel in your own safe place with party situations.

JOURNAL EXERCISE #2

Visualization exercises help you look realistically and positively at specific party situations. This exercise will help you apply what you've learned in your visualization exercises to your feelings about yourself.

1. As you complete each visualization, make notes in your journal about any thoughts or feelings you had during the exercise. Keep a record of your insights. You can go back and read it when you encounter a similar situation in real life.

2. Look at the list you made in chapter 8 of your good qualities, positive attributes, and achievements. Write each strong point about yourself on a different card, and carry the cards with you. Get in the habit of reading your positive I.D. cards just before a party or any other anxiety-provoking encounter.

3. Now, look at your list of weak points that you also made in chapter 8. How might your weaknesses affect your intereactions with people at parties? Can you do anything to prevent misunderstandings or negative interactions?

TAKING RISKS

Continuing avoidance behavior will keep us safe, but won't help us develop the self-esteem we need to enjoy ourselves with others. To gain confidence and a feeling of ease, we can begin by taking small risks at social events and achieve a measure of satisfaction. Progressive desensitization works because taking even the smallest step toward a goal increases self-confidence.

If the idea of going to a party seems overwhelming, the first step is to look at the party situation realistically and understand why it provokes so much anxiety. A party may actually involve complex elements that are beyond your present ability to control. But each of those elements are made up of small units that you can control.

From what you learned by mentally rehearsing your list of anxious party situations using visualization exercises, you can break down each situation into smaller parts and begin desensitizing yourself in real life. For example, you might have realized that one of your primary anxieties is making an entrance, which involves greeting friends and meeting strangers. It helps to set up a situation that allows you to practice only that, without the distractions inherent in a party.

Begin by introducing yourself to people who live in your building, or to people you see at work. After you feel comfortable with initial introductions, you might find a table in the lunch room where one or two people you don't know are already sitting. Eating lunch with people you don't know gives you a chance to practice conversation skills, as well as introduction skills.

If you feel uncomfortable about dancing at a party, you can begin by asking friends to go dancing one evening. Or you can invite friends to your place for a small dance session. You could also take lessons, which would provide another opportunity to meet new people.

When you feel comfortable with preliminary steps, it's time for the final step, attending a party. But you can smooth the way by incorporating some of what you've learned into the actual party. Instead of going alone, ask a friend along. Or you could invite a friend to have dinner first, then go the party together. As your confidence increases, you'll find that attending parties is a part of life you look forward to.

When you've learned to feel at ease at parties, you've accomplished something important because you've learned to feel comfortable around others. When you're comfortable, you enjoy people more, and you notice that people reciprocate by being more open and responsive. Even though your immediate goal was to conquer your anxiety at parties, the long-term result is that you feel better about yourself and about life.

PARTYGOING SKILLS

In chapter 6, we discussed Bobby, the boy whose parents tried to cure his shy behavior by forcing him to attend parties. Bobby's social anxiety became worse because he was unprepared to deal with the other children.

Even people who consider themselves comfortable in most social situations know how important it is to learn techniques for meeting and talking with people at a party. Accepting and asserting ourselves are the basic tools for dealing with any type of anxiety, but some specific techniques can be useful for interactions at parties.

As you practice your visualization and desensitization exercises, try using the following techniques at parties. You might not be aware that you lack some of these skills until you start using them!

Talking Tactics

Recognizing anxiety. One of the most important party skills you can learn is to recognize other people's anxiety. Everyone feels a certain amount of anxiety; all but the most insensitive people admit to some unease in social gatherings. When you help others become more comfortable, you forget about your own nervousness, and find yourself becoming more comfortable, too.

Starting conversations. If someone is standing alone, or sitting out of the way reading a book or magazine, chances are that person is too nervous to talk with others. Instead of focusing on your own feelings of anxiety, you can make a polite comment, introduce yourself, and wait for a reply.

"But I don't know how to start a conversation out of the blue!" you might protest.

Asking subjective questions. The easiest way to start a conversation is to ask someone a question. But before you ask, think about the response you're likely to get. If you want to get the other person to talk to you, don't ask something that can be answered in one or two words, or with a yes or a no.

Get the other person to reveal a little about themselves in their answer. Instead of saying, "So, you're from the City?" try, "What's it like living in New York?" Instead of asking, "How many children are in your family?" try, "How do you feel about large families?"

Concentrating. We don't usually know it at the time, but our party behavior often consists of polite smiles and automatic replies to others' comments. Rather than allowing ourselves to become involved, we contain anxiety by avoiding real communication.

When someone is talking to you, are you really listening? When someone asks you a question or directs a statement your way, do you think about what is being said?

You probably have a meaningful thought or feeling about the subject, even though your initial reaction might be to keep quiet and give a simplistic or conventional response. Try really expressing yourself, and see how quickly your anxiety decreases.

When you become involved in a stimulating discussion,

you make both mental and emotional connections. Instead of just taking up space, you can learn and teach and connect with others.

Behavioral Buttresses

Make eye contact. Making eye contact is an important part of involvement. If you find it difficult to look directly at someone you're talking to, ask yourself why.

Perhaps secret fears are lurking just beyond your conscious awareness? Perhaps you imagine that the person you're talking to is rejecting you? It's just as likely that the other person is exuding positive, encouraging energy. Wouldn't you prefer to know? If you won't look into the other person's eyes, you're mind-reading when you guess how they feel about you. Quite often, the other person is just as nervous as you are. Be brave. Make the first eye contact.

Arrive on time. Don't wait until a party is under way to make your appearance. By getting to a party at or close to the time it's supposed to start, you'll have less pressure to make a grand entrance. When you're one of the first to arrive, you have a chance to talk with the host and meet people before the place gets crowded and the pace intensifies.

Touch. When you want to make a connection with someone, don't be afraid to move physically toward them, and even touch them lightly and briefly on the arm. Touching another person can be relaxing and reassuring for both of you. Sometimes it feels even more positive to initiate the touch than to be touched.

If the person you're talking to is nervous about being touched, they'll let you know. Don't take it as a personal affront. Remember that being able to touch and be touched are special communication skills. If someone is not able to be touched, accept that without feeling it reflects on you.

Relax. Before you go to the party, or before your guests arrive, allow yourself sufficient time to relax. Use focused breathing or progressive relaxation. Call up your special sanctuary. Breath deeply and evenly as you move about the party and talk with people. Keep your positive I.D. cards in your pocket, and look at them whenever you have a chance.

Mental Magic

Suspend judgment. Don't go to a party with preconceived ideas about what will happen. Whether a party turns out to be a wild bash or an intimate evening is often beyond your control. Let yourself enjoy the unexpected.

If you're giving a party, don't welcome your guests with expectations for the evening. Don't set yourself up for disappointment by wanting certain people to do certain things. Relax and let the evening unfold.

Think realistically. If you find yourself feeling anxious, try to find the source of your symptoms.

Is it one of the four fears? Or is your thinking distorted? If you find yourself toying with unrealistic expectations, stop and put your mental anxiety away by putting the evening into perspective.

It's just a party, it's not a life or death struggle. Remind yourself that you are a unique individual, with strengths and weaknesses. The other people at the party have their own good and bad points.

You're there because you feel good about yourself and want to enjoy the pleasant experience of seeing and talking with other people. If you don't find the party enjoyable, you are free to leave.

Like yourself. If you find negative thoughts creeping into your mind, deal with them consciously. Are you wondering how other people think you look? Are you thinking that the attractive man across the room suspects you're trying to pick him up?

Tell yourself that you approve of the way you look. You don't need anyone else's approval, just your own. You can't expect everyone at the party to like you, anymore than you would expect yourself to like all of them.

There are some people at the party who you do like, and some people who also like you.

If you're not trying to attract the handsome stranger, remind yourself that you are not responsible for what he thinks. If you wouldn't mind meeting him, start a conversation. Or be friendly if he approaches you. What have you got to lose?

A lot of hidden agendas get enacted at parties. People go to parties to look for potential dates, potential mates, and to make work connections. An ulterior motive is not necessarily bad. Know who you are and why you're at the party, and don't worry about what other people are doing or what they think you're doing.

Make a game of it. If you find yourself resisting or avoiding a party or wishing you could leave because you have no one to talk with, make up a secret game for yourself.

Pretend you're a spy, trying to infiltrate this strange group of people. Or pretend you're a society reporter, writing an article about the party. Or pretend you're doing a scientific investigation about partygoing behavior. Let yourself have fun. Don't be surprised if you find yourself really enjoying the party before the evening's over.

Ultimate Party Techniques

Making mistakes. Perhaps the most important party skill we can learn is to remember that we all make mistakes. If we don't expect perfection, we are free to enjoy ourselves, without feeling the need to control the outcome.

Every remark we make won't be clever. Everyone we talk to won't be interested in us. But the realistic chances are that some of the people will be enjoyable, and some will enjoy your company. Talking to even one interesting person can make a party a worthwhile experience.

Recognizing pleasure. All of your efforts to accept yourself and relax need to be reinforced with your success. Allow yourself to recognize your pleasure and enjoyment. Notice how comfortable you feel, if not all the time, at least at certain moments. Make mental notes about what feels good. Later, you can write these notes in your journal.

For now, appreciate yourself for the work you've done, and recognize the progress you've made.

10 At Ease At Work

Man does not only sell commodities, he sells himself and feels himself to be a commodity.

ERICH FROMM

Anxiety in the workplace affects people at all career levels. Maybe you freeze when your supervisor scrutinizes your work, but did you know that many supervisors, managers, and CEOs admit that they too experience anxiety when they attend important meetings, when it's time to hand out reviews, or when they get their own reviews?

The stress caused by work anxiety is enormous, affecting productivity, work relationships, even health and personal relationships. Social anxiety in the workplace can hinder career growth by affecting your professional image, your self-confidence, and your ability to promote yourself. The time you spend at work makes up one third of your life, so you can't avoid dealing with work-related anxieties.

THE PROFESSIONAL IMAGE

Most of us would say that a professional image is important. But what exactly is a professional image? Is it something we wear, or something we assume, like a disguise? Does it become a permanent part of us, or is it something we use only at work?

To some people, being professional means being in power, so they wear power clothes, eat power breakfasts, and drive power cars. It's not hard to find books and private consultants to teach you power talking, power walking, and power body language.

Others view the work world as a playing field. To them a professional image depends on how well you do at the game, as in playing politics, corporate gamesmanship, and playing ball. At one time the name of the game was manipulation. A more recent favorite was assertiveness, which often meant slinging the hardest criticism, first.

Still others claim that nothing is as important to the professional image as appearance. Looking good and showing a positive attitude are considered career essentials. Many business counselors contend that the first impression will make or break a deal, a relationship, even a career.

The problem with all these well-established beliefs about professional image is that they focus on the person's surface. All of our time and energy is used to create a false image, designed to hide our true selves from the people with whom we work.

We already know what happens when we don't express ourselves freely. Can a superficial appraoch to work create anything but more anxiety? If we really believe in personal goals of openness, honesty, and freedom of choice, how can we condone the opposite in our work enviornment?

If we don't know what we feel and think about our job and our work environment, how can we present anything but a facade? If our professional image is not a true reflection of ourselves, can we ever truly achieve success?

CREATING OUR OWN IMAGE

A professional image is a tool we use to present our best selves at work. Being professional doesn't have to mean pretending to be someone we're not. We can express ourselves genuinely without abandoning career goals.

212 Always At Ease

By applying the lessons we've learned about self-esteem and self-assertive communication, we can explore our inner thoughts and feelings and learn what is really important to us in our working lives. Self-knowledge itself brings a feeling of accomplishment and personal power; the successful professional image we project will then reflect our true selves.

Creating Your Own Image: Karen

Karen's hard work and good grades in college helped her find a job shortly after graduation with a San Francisco advertising agency. She was nervous at first, but she told herself she'd get over it when she was no longer the new kid on the job. Instead, after her first year her anxiety increased, and she felt highly stressed at work.

The second year was even worse. Although her work was praised, Karen backed away from projects that required her to give presentations or to develop selling strategies. When she disagreed with a project plan, she kept her ideas to herself, and followed the directions she was given. She told herself she was a member of a team, not out to win glory for herself or compete with others. That year, Karen found out that two people who'd recently been hired had gotten hefty raises, while her salary stayed the same.

It often takes a major disappointment to force us to face the grinding anxiety we feel about our work. Karen felt that she deserved the reward she watched others receive. In her opinion, their only distinguishing quality was the ability to chat with higher-ups over coffee. Karen felt that she knew as much and was as good at her work as the new employees.

Despite her view of the situation, Karen had to accept that her agency saw things differently. But what did they expect of her? Karen felt that playing games to get raises and promotions was beneath her. She was willing to dress like the others, eat lunch with the others, and give her best to her work. But she refused to "play politics" to get ahead.

Karen felt caught. She wanted to advance in her company, but she felt increasingly uncomfortable with what she saw as the path to success. The escape from the trap was for Karen to evaluate her own thoughts and feelings. She needed to see herself realistically before she could begin to express her true self.

Karen began a program for dealing with work anxiety. Part of her homework was a journal exercise: she was to get in touch with her thoughts and feelings about work by examining her early family life. Karen had some interesting insights. Because she had grown up in a family that demanded conformity, she had never learned to feel comfortable expressing a different opinion.

It was her basic anxiety about being different, along with a fear of rejection, that prevented Karen from effectively expressing herself at work. Over the past two years, Karen's anxiety had grown almost to the point of incapacitating her, and she had not, until now, ever suspected the source of the problem.

Although she had wanted desperately to give her best, she really hadn't done that. Her anxiety had been so great that she'd held back original ideas and criticisms of others' work, while blaming her inability to contribute on her peers' game playing. Her new understanding helped Karen realize that she could participate and express her opinions, without feeling manipulative.

Knowing that the source of her anxiety was within her gave Karen a feeling of hope. She no longer felt frustrated by the behavior of the other people at the agency, because she felt better about herself.

JOURNAL EXERCISE #1

This exercise will help you put your fears about work into a realistic perspective. Remember to be as specific as you can. When you finish, look for patterns in your responses.

1. Make a list of the daily, weekly, or monthly aspects of your work that create anxiety for you.

2. Now ask yourself: what is the worst thing that could happen in each situation? Write down your thoughts, feelings, and fears, about each item.

3. Do you see any distorted thought patterns?

4. Can you counter any of your unrealistic expectations with realistic reasoning?

Here is Karen's list.

KAREN'S WORK ANXIETY LIST

1. I have to sit in a planning meeting every Monday. I often have ideas, but I feel too anxious to speak up and offer suggestions or make criticisms.

2. The worst that could happen: if I speak up, everyone might ignore me. Or if I present my idea, what if no one likes it? What if they laugh at me?

3. Distorted thoughts: I am obviously predicting-the-future by assuming the worst. I'm mind-reading when I guess what they'll think and how they'll act, and generalizing by expecting one meeting to determine my whole career.

4. Realistic views : even if the worst happened, so what? It doesn't mean I'm stupid, just because they might not praise every idea I have. And it happens to other people all the time. I can't expect everyone to like all my ideas all the time. But if I don't begin expressing them, I'll never have a chance to participate.

One of Karen's most important changes was her realization that involvement and participation didn't mean she'd have to compete. The idea of vying against others in the company was repugnant to her. Instead, she learned that she could make an honest contribution simply by expressing herself.

Karen's efforts to deal with her work anxiety had a broader effect on her life. She began to speak more honestly about her feelings and her ideas with her family and friends. She found herself feeling more connected to the people she cared about, because they responded to her honesty by being more open about themselves.

Karen learned that she did not have to change her beliefs to get ahead. By taking care of her needs, she no longer had to depend on financial rewards to validate her efforts. As she learned to value herself, Karen's self-confidence and willingness to contribute became apparent to others in the company, and she received their financial appreciation.

In many workplaces, office politics and portrayal of a superficial professional image dominate, simply because ambitious people try to duplicate their perception of someone else's successful strategies. Unless becoming a political animal is your ultimate goal, why spend your time learning how to be artificial, in hopes of pleasing others?

As Karen learned, the real reasons for work anxiety and job dissatisfaction comes from within. Only you know your goals. Only you know what will make you feel good about yourself.

THE IMPOSTER SYNDROME

Until Karen began dealing with her anxiety, she thought she was making her best effort. Then she began to understand the many ways she was holding back. For some of us the opposite is true: we don't consider our accomplishments to be part of who we are as people. Whatever we've achieved was the result of luck. You may be one of those people who live in secret fear that someday you'll be found out and exposed as a fake.

The imposter syndrome can impose real obstacles to your career goals. If you have difficulty asking for a raise or negotiating a good review, it may be that you can't accept your accomplishments as yours or yourself as competent.

If you find it difficult to discuss your achievements in front of others, if you sit silently while others are rewarded for work you did, if you feel that you're watching opportunities drift by, it may be your own inability to acknowledge your achievements that is holding you back.

The Imposter Syndrome: Steve

Steve had been senior manager of his electronics firm for four years. When the vice-president announced his retirement, Steve was called into the president's office. "The job is yours," Steve was told.

It was an exhilarating day. Almost everyone in the department came by to congratulate him. As he drove home, Steve planned where to take his wife for a celebration. But as soon as he opened his front door, a heavy mood descended on him. Instead of inviting his wife out, Steve went into the den by himself. He sat for two hours, contemplating the reasons he should turn down the job. He just couldn't see himself in the number two chair.

Steve was experiencing the imposter syndrome. In his mind, from the day he'd started 18 years ago, his success had all been a matter of luck. Steve had been offered his very first job in quality control, right out of college. His connection? The summer before, he'd met one of the company's managers when they both helped with the local baseball league. From then on Steve had been fortunate to work for good people who looked out for him. Eventually he'd been promoted to manager himself.

Now suddenly he felt trapped. How could he be vice-president? The promotion would put him in a position of great responsibility. he wouldn't be following orders anymore: he'd be giving them. How long would it take for everyone to realize he wasn't qualified? Would his incompetence be revealed before his decisions drove the company to bankruptcy?

ACCEPTING THE GOOD

For some of us, self-discovery comes when we hit a road block; for others it arrives with unexpected success. It is sometimes more difficult to accept what is good about ourselves than to come face-to-face with our faults. When we're not accustomed to recognizing our strengths and weaknesses, our value as individuals usually remains fuzzy in our minds, a tally that is forever intangible. But unlike other bottom-line totals, our personal worth is more than the sum of our parts.

During the whole of his career, Steve had spent almost no time defining his personal goals. Now he felt he was facing an abyss. He believed his own qualities had taken a back seat while his mentors had driven his career ahead. Steve's unrealistic opinion was based on his knowledge that he had never set out to achieve anything, but had still reached the top.

Steve asked for confidential help from a vocational counselor and began working on exercises to put his career into focus. His first task was to articulate the belief underlying his anxiety. Steve came up with this:

> "I'm a fake. The only reason I got to my present position is that others helped me. Soon the whole company will find out I don't know anything."

Being able to state the source of his anxiety proved a real breakthrough. He began by writing what he honestly felt, but as soon as his feelings were down on the page, he could see they were based on an unrealistic premise. In Steve's company, and with his type of work, no one, including himself, could continue to do the job without expertise. And what did his faulty premise say about his supporters, to think that they'd helped a fool get into a manager's chair?

After realizing his mistake, Steve wanted to examine his feelings of inadequacy. Just as if he were doing an inventory, Steve began to take stock of all his assets. It was a strange sensation, reviewing his past and recognizing for the first time that even though he had had support, it was his own talents that had been rewarded with each promotion and raise.

Another part of Steve's learning process was recognizing his fear of being put to the test. In the vice-president's chair, he'd be an important part of a policy-making team. In a spotlight that intense, any small mistake would be visible to the company. Steve realized that to succeed at the new job, he would have to accept his fear of failure.

JOURNAL EXERCISE #2

This exercise will help you close the gap between your self-doubt and your true personal value.

1. For an entire day, keep a list of everything you achieve, no matter how trivial.

2. Begin a weekly record of your accomplishments. Again, include even small details if they're important to you.

3. Make a list of your career goals. What do you hope to accomplish with your work?

4. Explore your feelings about your work. Do you see yourself as being on the right path to achieve your goals? Or, are you being pressured by others to get ahead or be more ambitious? How do you feel about your opportunities for the future?

THE AUTHORITY FIGURE

The anxiety brought on by interactions with managers, supervisors, or others in authority can cause tension and self-consciousness. The fear of authority can affect your success in dealing with those higher up or further along than you are. It can damage your self-confidence and lower your self-esteem. It may well reflect an inability to be responsible for yourself. Learning to interact with authority is a crucial part of any working situation.

Isn't the Boss Always Right?

Fear of authority often comes from misunderstandings about what authority means. If authority actually meant intrinsic power, a person in authority would have absolute control, just like the gods of mythology. Everyone else would be in an inferior position.

In the workplace, authority usually implies expertise. The word *authority* is derived from 'author; the mover, the creator.'

Authority is power, but a power based on respect, esteem, and honor.

A person with authority is someone who has the knowledge and experience to direct others. In actual practice, some authority figures do seem to prefer that underlings fear their power, rather than respect their knowledge. But sometimes the fear of authority is a false perception.

Fear of Authority: Allen

Allen experienced problems with three different manaagers in two large retail companies where he worked over a five-year period. His present job creates so much anxiety that Allen is considering moving again. Whenever he has to deal with his boss Meg, Allen feels like he's walking on eggshells. He actually holds his breath, hoping not to cause an argument, while he prays Meg won't say anything he'll have to disagree with.

Without being conscious of it, Allen assumed that his boss has absolute power over every situation. In his mind, disagreeing with her would have been the same as declaring war. Disagreements with supervisors forced Allen to leave two previous jobs under unhappy circumstances. In both cases, Allen acted from his fear of confronting authority. He never even tried to deal with the problems.

The best antidote for fear of authority is realistic thinking. Articulating fears brings unrealistic expectations and thought distortions to the surface. When Allen managed to express his anxiety by shaping his thoughts and feelings into a statement, the results surprised him.

Allen's statement was, "I must do whatever Meg says, no matter what, or I'm not a good employee."

Once he faced his fear, Allen was able to redefine his work situation. Why did he have to do everything Meg said? Would she want people under him to be so subservient? What would happen if he didn't follow Meg's orders? Would he be fired or sent to some backwater position?

Were there any objective facts to support Allen's feelings? Had Meg or any other supervisor confirmed his idea of their working relationship? Was there any reason to believe that Meg actually expected him to do whatever she said?

By using realistic thinking, Allen was able to come up with a new understanding of his situation. He began to test his new ideas and realized that Meg was open to other opinions, and in fact, expected him to disagree with her at times.

Most important, Allen now realized that he had a choice about his actions. If he decided to follow Meg's direction, that was his choice. If he decided not to, that was also his choice. As a responsible employee, it was his job to explain his thinking when he chose to disagree with Meg, or with others in authority.

Desensitizing to Authority

Allen learned to take responsibility for his opinions and actions by building his confidence with desensitizing exercises. First, he defined his goal: to express his ideas openly with Meg. Then, he created small, somewhat controlled situations that would give him the opportunity to practice in a safe environment.

Allen began with his family's weekly dinner gathering. He visualized himself expressing his opinion on a current event, and he imagined his parents and brothers and sisters and their families reacting with respect. Then, using breathing exercises to control his anxiety, Allen jumped into the fray during an actual family dispute. His family didn't stop arguing, but they took Allen's point of view seriously.

From that safe beginning, Allen went on to discuss minor issues with friends and people he knew at work. Then he began to participate at staff meetings, giving an opinion out loud, even when he agreed with the consensus. Next he spoke up in disagreement. And finally, he was able to accomplish his goal.

During the next department review, Allen suggested to Meg that his department could be organized differently. She listened quietly, then began scribbling on a pad.

Allen's heart pounded in his chest. He told himself that no matter what she said, even if she fired him, he felt good about himself. He had finally been able to tell her what he thought. He reminded himself that he was an intelligent person, and his suggestion was for the good of the company, not for his personal gain.

Meg looked up from her pad and said, "Thanks Allen. That might work." Allen smiled with relief. Then Meg surprised him. "You know," she smiled, "I've been trying to figure out how to solve the loss problem in that part of the store, and your idea gives me something to work with. I'm going to talk to the regional manager and get back to you."

Allen was able to accomplish all this because he was willing to define what was important to him. If collecting a paycheck every month had been his only goal, he might have continued doing whatever his boss said, because it would require less on his part. Instead, he wanted to make a contribution, and he was willing to accept the consequences of his actions.

At one time, Allen would not have believed that speaking out would lessen his anxiety. Now, he finds that he no longer feels anxious, but looks forward to work. Instead of dreading meetings with his boss, he looks forward to talking with her about problems and accomplishments, his own and those of others. Allen learned that taking responsibility is what creates a team spirit.

JOURNAL EXERCISE #3

This exercise will help you recognize blocked feelings that can create resistance when dealing with people in authority.

1. Think about a recent incident that left you feeling frustrated or anxious at work. Write down a brief description of what occurred.

2. Now, think about how you felt. Make a list, as you try to remember all the emotions you felt at the time. Include

any emotions you feel now, when you recall the incident in your mind.

3. Allow yourself to re-experience any bothersome emotions, like anger or frustration.

4. Now, write down what you'd like to say to your boss, or whoever needs to hear what you have to say. Write anything you want, just as though you were talking or writing a letter. This is not a letter that you'll ever send, but it is your chance to complain and let out the negative feelings you don't express in reality. This is your private gripe sheet and no one but you will ever see it.

5. After at least one day, reread your gripe sheet. Make any additional remarks you feel are important.

6. Continue the process of griping and reviewing your gripe sheets for a whole week. Write down any additional problems that develop. As the week progresses, you'll find yourself becoming more effective at expressing your true feelings.

WORKING WITH DIFFICULT PEOPLE

Some fellow employees will tease, criticize, or annoy you. In the work environment, you can't always avoid bothersome people. But not dealing with these unpleasant coworkers can provoke a great deal of anxiety.

You may think, "What can I do about it? It's their problem!" But in reality, if someone bothers you, it's your problem.

Think for a moment about any difficult people you have to deal with. Who has a hard time, you or they? Who feels the situation is difficult, you or they? Who ends up with the frustration and anxiety of repressed feelings?

By taking responsibility for your anxiety, you gain the ability to change the way you interact with the person who annoys you. No, you can't change another person, but you do have control over yourself. Instead of feeling frustrated, you can use your anxiety as a warning that something is wrong in one of your work relationships.

But Teasing Is Friendly, Isn't It?
In some cases, teasers think they're being friendly, using humor to create and develop a relationship. But people who tease often have their own problems, perhaps an inability to commuunicate directly. And sometimes teasing can be an aggressive, but indirect means of criticizing, like knocking someone down without having to acknowledge the punch.

Trust your emotions. If you feel that someone is teasing you in friendship, you might accept the teasing, and try teasing back. Ask yourself, does the teasing have a genuine humor behind it? Can you appreciate the truth behind the joke? Does the other person accept your teasing with a sense of humor?

If your emotions are signalling that a situation is not friendly, but hostile, then you need a different response. If the teasing is not humorous, don't laugh. If the teasing is painful, let the teaser know.

You can say, "You might think you're just teasing, but I feel uncomfortable about it." When you admit that the teasing is uncomfortable, you remove your tormenter's source of power.

What About Critics?
People who constantly criticize are more direct than teasers. Critics may feel that they are acting from a desire to be honest, that they just want to forge a good relationship. But like teasers, people who chronically criticize can't know how you feel about their harassment until you tell them. But don't react defensively. That gives power to your critic and usually intensifies your anxiety. The key to dealing with criticism is not assuming responsibility for the critic's thoughts or words. However, not assuming responsibility doesn't mean ignoring criticism.

Begin by responding assertively. This can take several forms. Instead of assuming that a criticism is negative, try to focus on any positive aspect of the critical remark. If you don't understand a criticism that is directed at you, don't be afraid to ask what is meant. Clarification of a critical remark can often change the context of the original delivery.

As Deborah Bright says in *Criticism in Your Life,* when you don't become defensive, you can use criticism as a springboard for identifying problems and finding ways to solve them.

Dealing with on-the-job criticism using the self-assertive communication techniques found in chapter 4 can feel awkward at first, but ask yourself: how good is the communicatin in your office now? Dealing assertively with criticism is an effective way to boost both your self-esteem and office morale.

What If Someone Is Just Too Friendly?
How do you feel about socializing with people from work? If a coworker asks you to come shopping at lunch time, or invites you to go for a drink after work, how do you respond? Do you lie to avoid spending time with the person, or do you take a chance and go?

Do you ever get together on weekends with colleagues and their families? Or, do you make it a habit to separate your worklife from your friendships?

Getting to know coworkers can be a rewarding part of any work experience. But making friends at work can stir up some basic doubts and fears. Whenever you turn down a friendly gesture or offer, ask yourself if you have a valid reason. Or are you simply avoiding the anxiety you'll feel if you become intimate with people you must see at every day work?

There's no reason why you can't turn down friendly offers if you're not comfortable accepting them, but it's good to be consciously aware of your reasons, especially when you decide not to pursue the possibility of a positive, friendly relationship.

Are you afraid of what your coworkers might think about your developing a friendship with someone at work? Maybe you believe that becoming friendly with someone could interfere with your work. Or are you afraid that you'll be perceived as less serious about your job?

When you're clear with yourself, you can be clear with the person whose offer you're refusing. Maybe shopping at lunchtime is simply not your thing; maybe you don't drink, or you don't like bars. Whatever you think, let the other person know. Practice asserting yourself by expressing your true feelings.

Letting the other person know that you find social situations difficult might help you deal with your fear of intimacy and start a friendship. Finding someone you can be open with at work may help you deal with tense situations that arise later on. Having a friend's support can also make work pressures seem less intense.

SALES ANXIETY

Most people who sell as a profession don't think of themselves as suffering from anxiety. Meeting and talking with people is the most enjoyable part of selling. Yet at times almost all salespeople admit feeling unsure of themselves and depressed at the prospect of facing another client.

If you sell for a living, you face the fear of rejection every day. Hearing endless no's, it becomes harder and harder to anticipate that all important yes. It's easy to slip into the distorted pattern of generalizing. After one negative transaction you feel that a whole day is shot. From one bad day, you assume you're on a downturn. A bad week can easily be projected into a disastrous season. One low monthly sales figure, and you label yourself a loser.

Soon you're looking at your record, not at your potential. Your confidence and self-esteem may surge with hope when you approach a new client, but fall apart when you don't make a sale. Or maybe you're flying high one day, and down in the dumps the next.

Perhaps you experience these emotional leaps and falls as your normal mode of existence, without realizing you are experiencing anxiety. Recognizing your anxiety and finding the source of your frustration makes it possible for you to develop a realistic, positive approach to your work. Sales anxiety is very much like other forms of social anxiety. The key is learning to accept yourself.

What is a positive, realistic approach in the world of sales?

Be honest about what you're selling. Are you selling a product, a service, or yourself? Use your assertive communication skills to let potential customers know what you offer, and learn to be assertive about asking your customer's intentions. If you know what potential clients want from the beginning, you can make an honest presentation of your services or your products. Why spend your time and energy trying to persuade people to buy something they don't want or need?

Be yourself. One of the most difficult anxiety traps of selling is the idea that you have to please the customer to make a sale. Phony compliments, overly optimistic promises, and inappropriate jokes are usually obvious, and don't make a customer feel any better than they make you feel.

Instead, focus on your client. Show your genuine desire to be of service by getting to know your customer as a person. At the same time, use your knowledge about your work to access your client's needs. Enjoy the proceess, whether you make a sale or not.

Be realistic. Every customer won't buy something every time, no matter what efforts you make. A negative transaction is not a reflection on your work, nor is it an indication of your worth as a person. you are more than your job.

JOURNAL EXERCISE #4

This exercise will help you gain realistic expectations about the art of sales work.

1. Take several slow, deep breaths. If you feel tense or nervous, give yourself time to use the focused breathing or the progressive relaxation exercises.

2. Call to mind your special sanctuary. Allow yourself a minute to enjoy the peace you feel in your own safe place.

3. Now visualize a selling situation that you face every day. Describe the situation aloud. Imagine yourself feel-

ing relaxed and in control as you speak honestly with your customer or client. Imagine that you feel comfortable, no matter what the customer's decison.

4. During an actual selling situation, monitor yourself, just as you did in the visualization exercise. Are you being your most genuine self? Are you being honest and open with your client or customer?

5. How did you feel after the actual situation? Did you feel more positive about yourself? Write down any feelings or thoughts you experienced.

6. Keep a list of several selling situations, especially those resulting in positive feelings. Describe what you did that helped you feel good.

7. Whenever you feel anxious about work, review your list of positive selling experiences. Repeat steps 1, 2, 3, 4, and 5 of this exercise.

TELEPHONE ANXIETY

Do you feel more anxious about using the phone than talking to people in person? Maybe your work requires you to use the phone, but you find yourself putting off important calls? Or do you make the call, but feel tense about it?

There are several reasons why you might feel anxious about using the telephone, but essentially, you are reacting to some fear about yourself, stimulated by the person on the other end of the phone. When you're not comfortable with yourself, calling someone can feel like an invasion, placing you in an apologetic, defensive mode. Without visual cues, such as facial expressions and body language, you might interpret a tone of voice as being more negative than intended. An awkward silence might seem like a rejection, rather than a simple pause or hesitation.

The feeling of being out of control can also be triggered by the ringing of the phone, since you're not able to control who's on the other end of the line. A ringing phone might remind you of negative experiences, like receiving bad news, being rejected, or simply being trapped into a lengthy conversation by an unexpected caller.

If you automatically feel annoyed when the phone rings, ask yourself *why*. As with other types of work-related anxiety, the key to dealing with the telephone is to be realistic about it. Unless every phone call you've ever had resulted in bad news, you're being unrealistic if you always expect something negative when the phone rings. There is just as much chance that a ringing phone means positive news.

When the phone rings, say to yourself that whether it's good or bad news, you appreciate being connected to another human being. Even if someone calls with a rejection, remind yourself that you were important enough for them to call you in person. And don't generalize. One negative phone call doesn't mean that you have to write off a whole relationship.

Learn to assert yourself on the phone. If you're really busy, let the person on the other end know that you want to talk to them, and set up a better time. When you make a call and the other person tells you they're busy, accept that. Then ask when would be a better time and set up an appointment to call again.

JOURNAL EXERCISE #5

This exercise will help you discover the source of the anxiety you feel about using the telephone.

1. Keep a record of any phone call that provokes your anxiety. Make notes about when the call was made, who called whom, what was discussed, and what you felt.

2. After a few days, compare notes from several calls. Make a list of specific factors that seem related to your anxiety.

3. When you next have to make an important phone call, relax by using breating and visualization exercises both before and after.

4. Develop a dessensitization exercise, so you can rehearse and become comfortable before your next major anxiety-provoking call.

JOB INTERVIEWS

A job interview usually feels like the ultimate in work-related anxiety. But in reality, a job interview is a more formal version of an ordinary social encounter. Instead of feeling powerless and scrutinized, you can learn to recognize and make use of the power that the formal interview gives you.

Instead of focusing on a particular interview, think about the entire process of finding a job. Why are you looking? What are you hoping to find?

If you're like most people, you know what type of job you want before you begin the search. But when it's time for the interview, all you can think about is how nervous you are.

Looking at a job interview realistically helps you see that it's an opportunity to find out whether a particular job is what you think it might be. An interview is a chance to meet people you might want to work with and to ask those questions that have been floating around in your head. The interview allows you to compare reality with your hopes about finding the right job. Until you interview a prospective employer, how do you know whether a particular job is what you hope it is?

> "That's easy for you to say, but I really need this job. If I don't get it, I'll starve!"

There are times when you might need a job to make money to pay bills, or to begin a career, or to pick up the pieces after some career disappointment. But there are almost no circumstances, no matter what type of work, no matter what position, when there is only *one* job. By thinking in win-or-lose terms, you set yourself up for unnecessary desperation.

> "How can I ask all my questions, and still make the best possible impression?

Whenever you begin to think about making an impression, you're doing yourself a disservice. The most valuable approach to any new situation is to be yourself. If what you really want is for people to accept you, you have to be willing to show your real self. Think of the job interview as an opportunity to find out if you would be comfortable in the new work environment with these new people.

> "But what if I don't know something they ask me? What if the other applicants have more experience than me?"

Being yourself means being comfortable with your present condition, while you continue to develop and improve. There is nothing wrong with responding to an interviewer's questions by saying, "I don't know." Interest and honesty are two invaluable qualities that a sharp interviewer won't overlook.

A job interview is a chance to show who you are, not to compete with other people. You won't be right for every job, just as every job won't be right for you.

JOURNAL EXERCISE #5

This exercise will help you incorporate relaxation techniques into positive, but realistic attitude about job interviews.

1. Take several slow, deep breaths. If you feel tense or nervous, give yourself time to use the focused breathing or the progressive relaxation exercises.

2. Call to mind your special sanctuary. Allow yourself a minute to enjoy the peace you feel in your own safe place.

3. Now visualize the upcoming job interview. Describe the situation aloud. Imagine yourself feeling relaxed and in control. Imagine that you feel comfortable asking questions and giving answers. You feel good about yourself, no matter what the interviewer's decision.

4. During an actual interview situation, monitor yourself, just as you did in the visualization exercise. Ask yourself these questions:
- Are you being your most genuine self?
- Are you being honest and open with the interviewer?

- Are you expressing your concerns assertively?
- Are you conducting your own interview to determine if you'd like the job that's being offered?

5. How did you feel after the actual situation? Did you feel more positive about yourself? Write down any feelings or thoughts you experienced.

6. Keep a list of your interviews, describing what happens and how you feel about each interview and each job. When an interview is positive, describe what you did that helped you feel good. If the interview was negative, what elements do you think determined the outcome?

7. When an interview you felt good about doesn't result in a job offer, review your reactions to be sure you were viewing the situation realistically. What, if anything, could you do next time to make the situation more positive?

8. Before your next interview, review your list of previous interview experiences. Focus on what made you feel good about yourself. You might make a list of what you've learned. Review any previous journal exercises that focus on your strengths and positive qualities. Remind yourself that you are a valuable person, and your decision to look for a new job reflects a realistic view of your future.

11 AT EASE IN PUBLIC

"Do as I do," said Dwight Eisenhower. *"I just transfer my nervousness to the audience . . . I look out at all the people . . . and imagine that everyone out there is sitting in his tattered old underwear."*

NORMAN COUSINS
"The Laughter Connection"
Head First

All the great speakers were bad speakers at first.
RALPH WALDO EMERSON

*I*f you don't like to get up in front of others to speak or perform, you're not alone; most members of the human race feel exactly the same. Even trained professionals are sometimes afflicted with terrible anxiety when they have to speak before an audience.

But what about less formal events, like talking to a group from your child's school? Or addressing the town council about a neighborhood project? Even being asked to make an informal presentation at work can evoke an enormous amount of anxiety in most of us.

Speeches and public performances are usually well-planned events that allow us time to practice and prepare, but almost always we feel more insecure in these situations than we do in those that are unrehearsed and spontaneous. When we are suddenly introduced to someone at a party, we are usually able to think on our feet and be polite, even charming or entertaining. Yet most people prefer that kind of stress to getting up in front of an audience and delivering a prepared presentation.

What is it about performing in public that ties our stomachs in knots and sends us into a turmoil of sleepless nights? Why is it that so many speaking experiences end with our firm resolve never to get up in front of an audience again?

MYTHS AND MISPERCEPTIONS

We've learned how our thoughts influence our feelings and how thoughts, when distorted, can cause unpleasant symptoms of anxiety. We can use what we've learned about anxiety to uncover our personal myths and misperceptions about speaking and performing.

I Have To Be Great, Don't I?
Many of us have special memories or deep feelings of reverence for great speakers. Some of us were awed by the eloquence of a hometown preacher, say, or the humorous speeches delivered by a high school principal. Others have been intimidated by historical figures like Abraham Lincolnn and more recently, John Kennedy and Martin Luther King, whose powerful rhetorical abilities influenced millions.

Whether we realize it consciously or not, hearing great speakers and watching fine performances make us expect the same qualities from ourselves. When we're asked to read a story to a group, we can't help comparing our narration to Garrison Keillor's. If we sing or play an instrument, we contrast ourselves to legends such as Julie Andrews, or John Lennon, or Pablo Cassals. How can we try to measure up to these stellar models and still feed good about ourselves.

The answer is we can't. But unless public speaking or performing is necessary for our careers, there is no reason to expect ourselves to have the eloquence, style, or timing of professionals. When we unconsciously compare ourselves to experts, we have difficulty approaching our own public appearances with realistic expectations—and unrealistic expectations are the source of our anxiety.

Instead, we need to learn to look at our own situation with honesty, not fantasy. Then we can overcome anxiety and actually begin to enjoy our opportunities to perform or speak in public.

Who are we speaking to? Why are we speaking? And what do we hope to accomplish? When we answer these questions, we begin to get a realistic understanding of our purposes. A realistic assessment is essential if we are to feel good about ourselves. Then we can concentrate on our true goals, whatever they may be.

All of us, no matter our previous experiences, can learn to appear before the public without feeling stiff or uncomfortable. We can learn the techniques of projection, so our voice is not harsh or strained. And we can prepare and practice our material until it is right for our particular audience. Practical goals like these are the key to overcoming anxiety.

But Isn't My Speech A Reflection of Me?
Some people feel that giving a speech is a formal test of their worth as a person, that their self-respect is on the line when they stand up to talk in public.

Molly—the physician we discussed in chapter 1—was comfortable and sure of herself in her office and with close friends, but when she was asked to speak to a community group, she found herself experiencing a considerable amount of anxiety. During her first talk on immunizations, Molly was so nervous that she mumbled through the first half of her material.

Halfway through, she managed to relax and complete her speech coherently. But when the audience began asking questions, Molly fell apart again. She ended up saying, "I'm sorry. I don't remember," and suggested that anyone with questions should call her office for more information. When it was over, Molly felt she had failed miserably as a public speaker.

Molly's over-reaction was the result of win-or-lose thinking. In her mind, the speaking engagement was critical to the expansion of her medical practice, and she had to perform eloquently to be a success. She hadn't been able to answer every question, so she generalized, labeling herself a failure.

Because Molly realized that speaking in public was essential to her career, she saw right away that she had to deal with her anxiety. She began by reviewing her first speaking experience, applying realistic thinking.

First, she listed the distorted thought patterns that had influenced her thoughts and feelings. Most obvious was the you must/you should thinking that controlled her expectations.

Next, she made a list of goals and purposes. In addition to her career goals, she listed the specific goals for her first talk. She'd been asked to provide information for parents about preventive medical care and the cost effectiveness of immunizations. Molly had prepared some comparative figures to illustrate her point, and though she brought along a list of the currently required immunizations, she had not thought to include recent incidence figures for all the diseases.

Her personal goal, she realized, had been to make a contribution to her community, and she had to admit that she had succeeded there. After her speech, several parents expressed an interest in bringing their children in for shots. In addition to her personal goal, Molly had achieved a professional benefit from her performance.

But Molly also had the unrealistic expectation that she should be a perfectly relaxed speaker, able to answer every question correctly. In her mind, her speaking ability reflected on her worth as a physician. In reality, the information she brought to the public was the most important aspect of her speech.

What if the worst possible scenario had happened, and

Molly had not been able to say a word? In reality, her inability to speak would not have destroyed her medical practice, nor affected her personal life. Molly's patients already knew her as a competent physician, and her friends and family knew her as a warm, loving person. Her ability or inability to speak in public wouldn't change their perceptions.

Separating feelings of self-worth from a particular action is a critical part of allowing ourselves to grow through new experiences. We all have potentials that will remain undeveloped unless we accept opportunities to explore life's vast possibilities. Unrealistic expectations set us up for failure and prevent us from trying.

The key to feeling comfortable before an audience is to recognize the part of ourselves that likes to perform, or inform, or entertain. Then we can give ourselves the support and encouragement we need to practice and learn.

But The Audience is Counting on Me!

A common misperception among novices in public speaking is that their audience is utterly passive until the moment comes to laugh and applaud, or upon failure, to boo and hiss. In reality, the audience, for the most part, wants to participate in the experience the speaker or performer is directing. People attend speeches or performances because they want to learn or laugh or be moved.

The best speakers achieved success because they are able to involve the audience in the emotion and purpose of their presentation. Remembering the purpose helps us see the audience not as distant, remote critics, but as interactive partners. Only then can we make the audience's response a part of our performance, not a judgment on it.

But They'll Be Looking At Me!

Even though we consciously understand the realities of speaking before an audience and do our best to prepare and rehearse, anxiety can develop from our unconscious and deep-rooted fears. A certain amount of generic anxiety is generated by any public appearance. When we're not aware of the cause of that anxiety, the effect can be paralyzing.

When we are the focus of public attention, we may feel we're being scrutinized like bugs under a magnifying glass. We imagine that each thread of our clothing will be subjected to intense inspection, as will every blemish on our skin. The slightest flaw will mark us as inadequate, no mater how well we know our material, no matter how smoothly we perform.

Making a realistic assessment and using relaxation techniques can help control rampant anxiety. We can remind ourselves that in fact, few people will see us up close, unless we're working an audience like Phil Donahue. Our hair and blemishes are probably not nearly as bad in reality as they seem to our anxious minds. But after we make these realistic reassurances, we still have to deal with the essential truth underlying our anxiety about our appearance.

When we're before an audience we are, *in fact,* what everyone will be looking at. Our image is often an important part of the message we want to convey. If we don't pay attention to our appearance, we ignore one of our most valuable tools for reaching the audience.

YOUR PERFORMANCE COSTUME

Paying attention to appearance is a positive way of dealing with performance anxiety. The following suggestions will help you put your generic anxieties into a productive framework.

Decide what image you want to convey. Two or three weeks before your speech or performance, think about how your image can help you get your message across. Do you want to appear sophisticated and authoritative, someone others can have confidence in? Or do you want to be accessible, warm, and friendly? Are you going to be talking with your peers, or are you appearing as an expert? Is the tone of the presentation serious, casual, or humorous? Do you want to blend in or stand out from the crowd?

Decide what you're going to wear. At least one week, preferably two weeks, before your presentation, select the clothing you will wear. If you need help, talk to friends, business associates, or the person who arranged for you to speak. Try on the clothes you select, including the shoes and any accessories you will wear, at least one week before the big day.

Do the clothes project the right image. How do you feel in them? Are they comfortable? Does anything need to be repaired, cleaned, or pressed? Don't wait; attend to the details now.

Be sure you have everything you need: socks, stockings, tie, belt, coat, possibly a hat. Don't forget you'll need a portfolio or attache case for your papers.

If you're not sure about the clothes you've selected, ask someone you trust to help you. Ask them to describe how you look; find out if they see the image you want to convey.

If you don't have the right clothes to accomplish your look, try to borrow something from a friend. If necessary, buy something appropriate. On special occasions, looking good is worth the investment, and you'll usually be able to wear the clothing again. Many department stores have professional helpers whose job is to help you find what you need, including an appropriate look for a specific occasion.

Trying to diet or to gain weight in time for your presentation is unrealistic. Have your clothes altered so they fit comfortably now.

Decide how you will wear your hair and if you will wear makeup. Are you comfortable with your hairstyle? If not, make any changes at least a week ahead of time, so you'll have time to adjust to the new style. If you plan to wear makeup, experiment ahead of time, and be sure you know just what to apply and how to apply it. Consider getting a professioal hair or makeup consultation if you're not happy with your current look.

YOUR PERFORMANCE STYLE

Perhaps the most important aspect of preparing yourself for any type of public performance is deciding what your message is and how you want to convey it. Then you can rehearse, using visualization and desensitization exercises. As you practice, try to be conscious of any feelings of anxiety, which can alert you that something about your upcoming presentation is not yet comfortable. Your goal is to practice, using mental rehearsals, until you can give your presentation with ease.

Rehearse material out loud. When you speak the words aloud, you'll probably notice some phrases that are difficult to say or will be confusing to the listener. Make changes, then practice the new version. Get a friend to listen and give you suggestions. Use an audio or a video recorder, so you can actually listen to yourself.

Practice your presentation. Whether you're giving a speech, presenting an award at a dinner, or offering a toast at a friend's wedding, go through the motions until you feel comfortable. Ask a friend to watch and make notes, or use a video camera so you can actually see yourself.

Practice as though you were really giving the speech or presentation. Notice how you feel. Are you standing or sitting? Are you stiff, or slumped over the podium? Does your clothing pull or twist uncomfortably? Do your glasses slide down your nose? Does your hair fall in front of your face? Make whatever changes are necessary to avoid any bothersome distractions.

Check to see if you have bothersome tics or mannerisms. While you're talking, do you unconsciously put your hand in front of your mouth, or rub your chin, or scratch your head? Find a place to put your hands, so you can become conscious of them. Allow yourself to be natural, but be aware of nervous gestures that detract from your presentation.

A REALISTIC APPRAISAL

Even after you've practiced and received feedback from a videotape or a friendly critic, you might feel another wave of anxiety. Don't ignore this improtant message. Use your journal or visualization exercises to help you focus on the less obvious aspects of the event that still make you uncomfortable.

JOURNAL EXERCISE #1

This exercise will help you recognize unconscious sources of anxiety. Remember to be as specific as you can. When you are finished, look for patterns in your responses.

1. Write a paragraph, describing how you *want* your speech or presentation to unfold. Give as many details as possible. Include how you want to feel before, during, and after the presentation. Describe how you want the audience to respond.

2. Now write a second paragraph and describe how you *realistically* think the presentation will go. Include how you think you'll feel, and how you think the audience will respond.

3. Compare the two paragraphs. What do you *want* to happen that you don't think will happen? Is what you want realistic? Can you seé a source for your anxiety in either of your paragraphs?

For example: you want the audience to give you a standing ovation and throw gold coins, but realistically you think they'll applaud politely. Your realistic paragraph shows that you are in touch with reality, while what you want is unrealistic, creating some anxiety.

Or: you want the audience to understand you, sign a petition, and join your group, but you think your accent will be a problem. Your realistic assessment is pointing to a factor that might make you less than effective.

4. Use your comparison to make a list of anxiety triggers that you can begin to deal with now. For example, if you have an accent that is difficult to understand, you could take speech classes, or work with a speech coach. You could ask a friend to evaluate your speech as you rehearse. You might learn that your accent is not as much of a problem as you think.

5. List possible solutions for any problems you foresee. For example, if you can't take speech classes, you can make a conscious effort to speak slowly, so the audience will more easily understand you.

ASKING FOR HELP

A friend who is willing to help you prepare for a speech or presentation can be a great help. Another person will see and hear things you're unaware of, and an objective point of view can help you evaluate details, including your message, your voice, and your appearance.

It's crucial that the person you select is someone you trust. You want to ask someone who is familiar with the type of presentation you're preparing for, so the advice they give will be appropriate. You also want someone who understands your feelings, who can give you both an honest critique and positive reinforcement.

Don't be afraid to tell your helper to be gentle with the criticism. It's easier to take diplomatic, compassionate advice. Criticism given in a positive way is just as effective, if not more so, than negative remarks.

FEELING COMPETENT

Feeling confident in your knowledge of the subject you're speaking about is essential for overcoming performance anxiety.

> Walter is a high school principal who frequently speaks before groups of parents at both school and community functions. He was recently asked to speak to a woman's group about a new study that would compare different ways girls and boys learn.
>
> Walter accepted the invitation, then became a nervous wreck. The learning study was so new. What could he tell these women? He had been a consultant on the project, but he wasn't really qualified to discuss the study design. "Who am I to give this talk?" Walter kept thinking.
>
> When Walter had accepted the offer to speak to the women's group, he was excited by the prospect of getting support for the new study. The women's group was very

influential, and Walter hoped his talk would result in their supporting the educational changes he hoped to introduce at his school.

But then Walter's anxiety kicked in. He worried about presenting statistics from the new study effectively. He felt inadequate, because he was just a consultant, not the primary researcher. The more Walter thought about the speech he was going to make, the more he felt like a fraud.

Trying to ignore all the negative thoughts in his head only made things worse. The week before the presentation, he felt paralyzed. Fortunately, Walter understood that he had to practice, so he asked Mrs. Benedict, a faculty member and his friend, to observe and critique him.

Mrs. Benedict recognized Walter's anxiety. She suggested a method she had used in a similar situation, writing down thoughts and feelings about the upcoming speech.

First Walter wrote down everything that had been tumbling around in his head, including his fear of being uncovered as a fraud. Then he made a list of the reasons he had accepted the women's invitation. Mrs. Benedict suggested he also include why he thought the women had asked him to give the presentation. Next, Walter made a list of all the reasons he shouldn't be speaking on this subject to this group.

In comparing his lists, Walter could see that although he was not the leading authority on the subject, he did have some information and exciting possibilities to tell the women's group. And more important, he realized, the speech would help him accomplish his goal of getting the women's group involved, so the curriculum could be changed more quickly.

After writing down his thoughts and feelings, Walter learned that some of his anxiety was related to yet another fear. Although he was comfortable speaking with parents, Walter had thought of the women's group as an unfamiliar audience; he'd labeled them as "different." Realistic thinking helped him acknowledge that many of them were parents of his students, women he had known for years, women who shared his concerns.

Anxiety about competence may be a signal that we need to do more work to be effective. When Walter realized that he did have something valuable to say to the women's group, his anxiety diminished. He was able to manage the rest of his nervous feelings by working on his speech and practicing his presentation.

SUGGESTIONS FOR EFFECTIVE SPEAKING

Ask yourself if you know all there is to know about your subject. Whether you've been asked to give a talk or whether you volunteered to lead a seminar or presentation, there are probably some aspects of the topic on which you're less than an expert. Talk to people who are experts and get their advice. Read as much as you can, and keep a file of information. And give yourself plenty of time to organize your material.

Prepare a defense. If you're going to be representing an argument or cause, learn the opposition's position. Can you support your view with details and examples? Prepare responses to questions you might be asked.

Be organized. Plan your presentation in terms of points you want to make. Organize your position, creating the most effective order for your material. Once your main points follow logically and dramatically, fill in the details. List each of your main points on a separate card, and rehearse your speech using the cards.

Practice, but don't memorize. Unless you're a professional, word-for-word memorizing can be tricky. You can sound too mechanical, or you can forget an important line without realizing it. When you are familiar with what you want to say, a one word clue written on a card will help you remember your point.

THE POWER OF POSITIVE REINFORCEMENT

A positive experience provides the best foundation for speaking or performing in public with ease. Completing one successful speech or performance provides realistic proof that we're capable. Even after bad experiences, a success has the power to override negative memories. With each additional success, we feel less threatened, and soon we begin to look forward to the next opportunity.

Remembering good experiences helps develop a positive, yet realistic, frame of mind. Instead of worrying about our anxious feelings, we are able to devote our full concentration to preparation and rehearsal. We're more open to criticism, less sensitive to the negative aspects of our performance, and more flexible about changing. We feel poised and confident before and during the speech or performance. And the performance itself becomes an enjoyable experience.

"Buy how do I create the first success?" you might wonder.

The best place to start is within yourself, by visualizing a successful performance. Once you've conquered your anxieties using visualization, mental rehearsals, and realistic, positive thinking, you'll be ready to move on to the real thing, using desensitization exercises. When the time arrives to give your speech or performance, you'll have built up the strong personal resources of confidence and positive reinforcement.

JOURNAL EXERCISE #2

This exercise will help you organize your concerns about speaking and performing, so you can plan a visualization and desensitization program.

1. Make a list of at least ten situations involving speaking in public that cause anxious feelings or other symptoms of anxiety. Include situations that provoke both low and high levels of anxiety. Here are some examples:

- Asking someone at a bus stop what bus to take.
- Proposing a toast at a family dinner.
- Making a political statement at a dinner party.
- Talking to school children about your job.
- Giving a presentation at work.
- Addressing an international group of your peers.
- Making an appearance on television.
- Acting in your community theatre.

2. Now, go back and rate each situation for the amount of anxiety you feel thinking about it, using a 1 for slight feelings of anxiety, a 2 for noticeable feelings of anxiety, and a 3 for severe feelings of anxiety.

3. Rewrite your list, so that all the situations you rate 1 come first, then all the 2s, followed by any you rated 3. Remember that situations rated 1 and even some rated 2 reflect fairly normal levels of anxiety for public speaking.

VISUALIZATION EXERCISE #1

You're now ready to use your imagination to overcome your anxiety in the performance situations you've listed.

Begin with a situation you rated 1 or 2. Gradually, over several days or weeks, you'll feel lcomfortable enough to move onto the 3s.

1. Sit or lie down in a comfortable position in a place where you will not be interrupted for at least ten to fifteen minutes. Loosen any tight clothing: belts, ties, collars, shoes. If it make you feel more relaxed, take off your glasses or contact lenses.

2. Take several slow, deep breaths. If you feel tense or nervous, you might want to begin with the focused breathing or the progressive relaxation exercises.

3. Close your eyes. Now, call to mind your special sanctuary. Allow yourself a minute to enjoy the peace you feel in your own safe place.

4. With your eyes closed, state out loud the scene you're going to create today. For example, making an appearance on a television show. A group you belong to is being featured in a news segment, and you've been asked to be the spokesperson. Say aloud, "I am giving my statement about the group to the news."

5. What is your goal? Your goal might be to present your group as exciting and innovative, because you want to attract new members. Or, your goal might be to let your community know about the hard work your group is doing, so you can get funding.

6. Imagine each step you make in achieving your goal.

- You prepare your statement.
- You contact the reporters you'll be talking to and explain that you want to be prepared. You tell them what subjects you want to cover and find out what questions they might be asking.
- You prepare answers to the reporter's questions and to others you think might come up in the interview.
- You select your clothing and dress with time to spare.
- You get to the news station early, review your notes, and relax.
- When it's time for your interview, you feel comfortable and relaxed. You know exactly what you want to say. The reporter asks questions you're prepared to answer.
- When your segment of the news is over, you thank the reporter and the people at the station, and leave. You feel good about yourself and your efforts.

7. See yourself breathing slowly and evenly as you imagine each step. Is your body relaxed? Monitor your feelings. Do you feel good about your efforts? Recognize your courage for confronting this difficult matter.

8. When you've accomplished your goal, let the exercise fade away. Call to mind your special sanctuary. Allow

yourself a minute to enjoy the peace you feel in your own safe place.

9. Before you open your eyes, notice your breathing. Is it slow and even? Does your body feel relaxed?

10. Now open your eyes. If you don't feel that you acheived a total state of ease, plan to repeat the same scene for your next exercise. You may want to increase your exercise time; give yourself long enough to visualize and be comfortable with the entire performance.

As you complete your visualization exercise, make notes in your journal about any thoughts or feelings you had while you were imagining yourself in each situation. Keep a record of your insights, so you can reread it when the time comes to practice the situation in real life.

It's important to monitor yourself as you practice the visualization exercises. If you feel any discomfort, use focused breathing or progressive relaxation until you feel in control. You might discover that a situation you had rated with a 1 actually provokes more anxiety than you anticipated. Feel free to move the situations around on your list. Come back to a difficult one, after you've successfully visualized the ones that provoke less anxiety.

As you begin to visualize giving an entire public speech or performance, your exercise session may take an extra twenty to forty minutes. Allow yourself enough time to complete the exercise, without feeling rushed or being interrupted.

Be sure to begin and end each exercise with positive, peaceful feelings, by calling up your special sanctuary. Remember that the positive feelings you evoke in your mental rehearsals will be powerful assets when it's time to accomplish your goals in reality.

USING PROGRESSIVE DESENSITIZATION

When you've reached a state of complete ease in your mental rehearsals, you're ready to approach the situation in real life. If you're dealing with a complex situation, like making a television appearance, you might want to begin by creating small scenes that allow you to approach the situation in stages. You want to be comfortable with each of the preliminary steps well in advance of your appearance.

For example, if you've been asked to be a spokesperson for your group on a television news show, you may have no control over the scheduling of your appearance. But if you can, try to set the date far enough in advance that you'll have time to practice and be comfortable with each step, without feeling pressured.

Your desensitization plan would include a practice session for each step that provokes any symptom of anxiety. Perhaps, for you, calling the reporter feels difficult. You could begin by calling a friend, instead. You would call and actually discuss the upcoming presentation, as though your friend were the reporter. You would ask questions and get your friend's input. When you completed that step comfortably, you would be ready to call the real reproter.

Perhaps the idea of speaking for your group is exciting, but you've never been on television. Maybe the idea of being in front of a television camera creates a lot of tension. You might include in your desensitization plan a preliminary visit to the television studio. Ideally, you would observe the news show on which you'd be appearing.

If you visited the studio at least one week, preferably two, before your appearance, you would have time to use your observations for mental rehearsals and practice with friends. You could arrange to have a friend videotape you as you give your presentation. You could ask another friend to pose as the reporter and ask questions.

DESENSITIZATION EXERCISE #1

This exercise provides a format to help you approach the actual speaking engagement or performance with ease.

   1. Take several slow, deep breaths. If you feel tense or nervous, give yourself time to use the focused breathing or the progressive relaxation exercises.

2. Call to mind your special sanctuary. Allow yourself a minute to enjoy the peace you feel in your own safe place.

3. As you approach the situation you've chosen to accomplish in real life, or a preliminary aspect of it, continue breathing slowly and evenly. As you walk up to the podium, or stand in front of the microphone or camera, think consciously about how far you have come. Remind yourself that you are well-prepared and confident about your abilities.

4. During your speech or performance, monitor your physical sensations and emotions. Is your breathing slow and even? Are you relaxed and comfortable? If you feel any kind of tension, take a deep breath. Remind yourself that you know and accept yourself as you are. Let yourself really appreciate the hard work that got you this far.

5. As you bring your speech or performance to a close, try calling your special sanctuary to mind. Allow yourself a minute to enjoy the peace you feel in your own safe place.

6. After your speech or performance is over, allow yourself to feel proud of your efforts. You have every reason to feel good, because you've just dealt with your anxiety in the most real way.

It's important to monitor your symptoms of anxiety before, during and after your speech or performance. If at any time you feel that any symptom is beyond your control, allow yourself to withdraw.

It's not as easy to excuse yourself when you're the guest of honor or performer, but it can be done. Tell someone in charge that you feel ill and need a moment to be alone. If that won't work, explain that you must take care of an emergency.

Go someplace where you can be alone and practice your relaxation exercises. Call up your special sanctuary and refer to your notes about your successful mental rehearsals. If possible, go through one more rehearsal of the speech or performance you are about to give. Try to determine the source of your anxiety, so you can address it with realistic thinking.

Remember that a temporary withdrawal is not a sign of defeat, but a way to increase your control over yourself. If you've been honest with your visualization homework, you are ready to face reality. With some positive reminders to yourself, you'll regain your confidence and be able to continue.

As you begin speaking and performing in real situations, try to keep a record of each experience. As soon as you're alone, make some notes about the way you felt before, during, and after your presentation. Be sure to record your positive reactions, as well as any negative ones. Your accomplishments deserve as much attention as the obstacles you face in reaching your goal.

If you're not completely comfortable with an experience, you will probably need to repeat it before you move on to a more difficult or complex situation from your list. Perhaps you've been asked to give a presentation to your company, and you decided to practice by presenting the material to your department first. If you weren't comfortable during that presentation, you could arrange another small presentation before you go on to the big one.

Some situations may take several attempts before you complete every step comfortably. Your goal is to keep practicing until you feel a real sense of pleasure from speaking or performing. By dealing with your anxiety head-on, you create a strong feeling of strength you can call upon in the future.

GETTING THE SUPPORT YOU NEED

At some point in your progress, you may realize that you need help that is not available to you in your everyday life. You might consider joining one of the many clubs or programs created to provide people experience with public speaking, such as Toastmasters.

You might also join a less formal support group of people like yourself, who want to improve their public presentation skills. If there's no such organization in your area, you could organize your own group.

Organizations and groups don't help you deal with your

anxiety directly, but they do provide a safe place for you to practice. You have an opportunity to present a speech with a safety net, because the people in the audience are dealing with the same concern as you are.

Even though you're talking to a support group, you're still practicing real public speaking. You hone your skills and gain self-confidence at the same time. You practice walking up to a podium, you listen to applause, you look out at a room full of faces. It's a great way to rehearse, because you always know that if you feel uncomfortable, you don't have to continue.

Practicing public speaking in a group setting also helps reinforce the positive progress you're making, because you have no other purpose and no end product to focus on. Being able to rehearse in such a supportive atmosphere gives you a chance to acquire real positive feedback before you tackle a less controlled situation.

PUBLIC SPEAKING TECHNIQUES

Whether you decide to join a group, or whether your visualization and desensitization exercises prepare you sufficiently, you will want to familiarize yourself with techniques that remind you of what you've learned. As you develop your own style, you'll be able to adapt the techniques to suit your needs.

Relax. Before and during any public performance, relaxation is essential. Tension creates a tight expression, a harsh tone of voice, and a rigid body. The audience can sense your tension, and they will reflect it back to you, creating a negative cycle. You can use relaxation exercises and visualization, even in the middle of a presentation, to achieve a tension-free state.

Warm Up. A speech or public presentation is a performance, and all performers know the benefits of warming up. Stretch and move your body to release physical tension and prepare for the event. Don't forget to exercise the focus of attention—your face—by practicing different expressions in front of a mirror. Warm up your voice with humming or singing. Recite a poem, varying your vocal inflection.

Accept Yourself. Anxiety specialist Dr. Claire Weekes, author of *Hope and Help for Your Nerves* and *Peace from Nervous Suffering*, points out that a mild level of anxiety is an entirely natural response; it is the flow of adrenalin anyone feels before making a presentation to others. But when you are anxious about your anxiety, your symptoms escalate, and you create an increasing cycle that can lead to intense anxiety and panic.

Remember that some anxiety is natural, and accept your nervous feelings. Remind yourself that you have chosen the experience you are about to undertake. You are in control. Your feelings of anxiety do not make you less of a person, or less competent a performer. Accepting your anxiety is the first step in putting it in second place to the exciting experience you are about to face.

Keep Your Head. Feelings of nervousness create a great temptation to use depressants, such as alcohol, or stimulants, such as nicotine, sugar, and caffeine that create even more tension and anxiety. Using tranquilizers is dangerous, because instead of dealing with the cause of your anxiety, you're masking your symptoms temporarily and artificially. The false sense of security can lead you into difficult situations that you're not emotionally or mentally prepared to handle.

When you rely on any substance to change your mental or emotional condition, you prevent yourself from experiencing your real thoughts and feelings. You don't allow yourself a chance to try out a new situation and grow.

Center Yourself. Any symptom of anxiety can distract you from the message you're delivering, or you can lose your focus in the excitement of the presentation. Create a subtle gesture to remind yourself who you are and why you are giving the presentation. Create a subtle gesture to remind yourself who you are and why you are giving the presentation. One expert finds that putting her thumb and forefinger together helps her feel anchored in the moment.

Watch Your Body Language. An open posture gives the audience the sense that you are comfortable with yourself, which makes them open and accepting in return. Don't cross your arms or legs or stand or sit rigidly. You need to make a conscious attempt to connect visually with the audience.

Keep Thinking. Some speaking situations require more than a well-prepared delivery. If a question-and-answer session follows your presentation, you'll need a broad knowledge of your subject. You could also be asked to lead an open discussion, which invites opposing points of view. Whether you're speaking at a political rally, at a stockholder's meeting, or at a high school sex education class, you need to keep thinking as you speak.

Radio and television interview shows provide great examples of thinking presentations. Instead of making a pronouncement, the interviewer involves the guest and the audience in a lively debate. The more who participate, the more successful the discussion, even though many points are made and no single solution is reached.

Professional interviewers are experts at deflecting negative or extraneous comments. If you're going to give a presentation to a less than receptive group, you might want to watch a variety of interview shows and observe different techniques for turning hostile comments into helpful points. Here are some deflection strategies:

- Come prepared with some humorous anecdotes involving yourself or someone known to your audience. Humor can break down barriers and relieve tension.
- Keep in eye contact with the audience. You'll be able to read positive, neutral, and negative expressions and

behavior. Don't feel that you have to avoid the negative voices, but don't hesitate to call on people who support your view.

- Assert yourself whenever necessary to keep the discussion under control. By saying, "That's an interesting point. I wish we had time to go into it in more detail," you can turn off a hostile remark without offending anyone.

- Acknowledge the value of other people's views, even if you disagree with them. "I was hoping someone would ask that question," is a response that supports the audience's right to express themselves, but also keeps you in control.

- Don't hesitate to admit when you don't know. You are not expected to be able to answer every question. You might ask if anyone in the audience knows the answer, and if no one does, acknowledge, "That's a good question. I hope you'll let me know the answer when you find out."

- Remember that the tension created by disagreements is not a reflection on you. If you can acknowledge different points of view, while presenting your own, you are a strong person.

Create A Bond With Your Audience. Learn as much as you can about each audience you address. Tailor your material to fit the needs of a particular group. Include jokes or humorous anecdotes that involve yourself and members of the group, or that pertain directly to the group's purpose.

Before you begin speaking, introduce yourself, so the audience knows who you are and why you are addressing them. Include personal information about yourself if it's relevant to the audience and to your presentation.

In addition to making yourself real, think of the audience as a group of friendly, familiar faces. Jerilyn Ross, president of the Anxiety Disorders Association of America explains that her secret is to pretend she's talking to people in her own living room. Invent your own method for making yourself feel good and positive about the people to whom you are speaking.

Use whatever physical methods help you feel comfortable. Take the microphone off the stand, remove the podium, get the audience to form a circle. With each speaking experience, you'll become more familiar with your own presentation style. Experiment with different styles until you find yourself feeling relaxed, and until you can sense that your audience is also relaxed and comfortable.

Remember that the audience has come to see you. They want a good experience, whether they agree with you or not. Just as you have learned to accept yourself, you can create a positive atmosphere by accepting your audience. When your presentation comes to a close, both you and your audience will have a positive experience to remember.

EPILOGUE:
PUTTING OTHERS
AT EASE

*Each of us really understands in others only those feelings
he is capable of producing.*

ANDRÉ GIDE

S hyness is not simply a personal loss, it is a loss for all of us. Every time someone holds back an idea at a business meeting, slips out of a party, avoids the chance to make a new friend, or turns down an offer to address an audience, we all lose. Vital ideals, great conversations, unique opportunities for new and perhaps deeply satisfying relationships have been forever lost. We all have something unique to offer the world: our selves. When we hold back who we are, our life and our world are diminished by what we might have given it. Yet, we are also diminished by what others may be holding back from us if they, too, are afraid. The willingness to help someone else, to be sensitive to the social anxieties of others, is a vital step not only in personal growth, but in making a small but significant contribution to creating a healthier society.

One motivation is simply to make *yourself* feel more at ease in the process. As H. L. Mencken said, "A large part of altruism, even when it is perfectly honest, is grounded upon the fact that it is uncomfortable to have unhappy people about one." Regardless of your motive, you'll find that if you try to put someone else at ease, you'll end up by putting yourself at ease as well.

WHERE TO START

It is, of course, one thing to say you would like to help put others at ease in social situations, but just what do you do? You don't want to be condescending or seem like an obnoxious do-gooder, nor do you want to simply take a wild and unskilled shot at it and perhaps worsen the situation. The best approach is simply a sincere and caring one, keeping in mind the ideas explained below. Reaching out to someone you sense is shy is a good thing, both for you and for the other person. You want to make sure that if you're willing to try, you can do it effectively.

First, you may wish to consider which people in your life you may want to reach. Here are some candidates.

- Someone at work who has a fear of giving presentations or speaking in public.
- Someone you have a crush on, and who may return the feeling but be too shy to acknowledge it.
- A parent whom you'd like to feel closer to.
- Strangers you meet in your everyday life.
- Neighbors who seldom speak to you or even wave.
- A boss who doesn't seem to acknowledge you.

PUTTING OTHERS AT EASE

Remember that feelings of anxiety indicate that a high level of value is being placed on the situation. Here are five specific things you can do to help put others at ease:

- Express your own insecurities in a self-accepting way.
- Touch the person—if you know them well enough—in a reassuring manner.
- Present a relaxed and friendly manner.

- Make gestures that give the other person a feeling that he or she is being included without pressure speak or perform.
- Make validating statements to the other person that indicate your approval and acceptance of them.

Expressing Your Own Insecurities

Let me recount a personal story to illustrate this first suggestion. Several years ago I was in Tulsa to give a talk and decided to go to the opening night of a local opera performance. I enjoyed it immensely and wanted to attend the reception following the performance even though I would not know anyone there and would be going alone.

When I got in the elevator and again as I walked toward the restaurant door, there were couples and groups of people chatting and laughing; people who knew each other. I wanted to turn around and leave. After all I had enjoyed the opera; I didn't need to attend the banquet. "No," I said to myself, "you're not going to chicken out. You might meet someone."

As I got in line for the buffet I looked around the elegant room and still saw only couples and small groups, all laughing and talking. "Where can I sit?" I asked myself. "I'll have to stand up in the corner somewhere all alone." I began to panic but then stopped by simply trusting that whatever happened, it would not be the end of the world and that I certainly wasn't doing anything inappropriate. After all, I was a stranger in town and didn't know anyone, and I was confident enough of myself that I hadn't just run back to the hotel, ordered room service and watched TV for the rest of the evening. I had really gone out and made the most of my opportunities.

With this small dose of realistic thinking I made it through the buffet and turned toward the room of tables, hoping that no one would see the sudden return of panic I felt as I searched for a hospitable place to sit down. I noticed that there was one long table across the back of the room. At first I thought perhaps it was the speaker's table but it did not seem set up that way. I decided to go ahead and give it a try.

As I slowly walked through the crowd of chattering couples, I noticed that at one end of the long table was an attractive woman sitting alone. My first thought was that her husband or boyfriend would be right back. Nonetheless, on impulse, I said to her, "You seem to be as alone here as I am." She smiled gratefully and said "Yes."

She turned out to be extremely interesting and we were the last two people to leave the reception. We both had a wonderful time and I will never forget my lesson in social risk-taking. Perhaps it was because standing there, alone, with my plate in my hand and no place to go, I took the risk of speaking to someone who caught my attention; but the result was that it put that person as much at ease as it did me.

The point is that you can often open conversation with a socially anxious person by first admitting your own insecurities. A sincere statement about how you feel may very well allow the person to accept his or her own feelings of anxiety, and respond warmly to your interest.

This is not to suggest that you approach someone and blurt out, "I used to be a total wreck at these kinds of events too, but I got over it." Clearly, a little tact is called for. You might say, "I always get edgy at these events, but I figure everyone else does also." The idea is to reach out in a sensitive but genuine way to let the other person know that you too feel ill at ease in such circumstances.

Touch
Touching people to comfort them can be tricky but it is still a good way to reassure a socially anxious person with whom you are familiar. What's important is not to touch in such a way that it seems you are feeling sorry for them because they are uncomfortable. A lingering touch or squeeze can suggest this. This may make them feel worse, especially if they are trying their best to put up a good front.

The best kind of comfort is a light touch or two as you are talking, or a brush on the arm as you leave. The touch should never be the focus of your interaction, but rather a genuine and friendly reassurance that you approve of them.

Presenting a Friendly Manner

People who are anxious are indicating that the experience has value to them; we do not get anxious in situations if they are trivial to us. Therefore, a person who seems aloof, shy, or distant at parties may actually be giving it more importance than the person who moves around talking to everyone and feeling completely comfortable. The anxious or shy person gives an unhealthy amount of weight to the event and to themselves.

Given this, you can use a positive and friendly manner to help demonstrate to the person how to put the event into a more realistic perspective. You might say, for example, "This kind of party is great since you don't have to worry about what you say. It's just friends, and it's okay to relax and be ourselves." Or, "I hate stuffy parties; the main thing is just to see each other." "I always feel a little uptight at these things at first—then I relax and have a good time." "I used to feel nervous at parties but the more I go to them, the more comfortable I feel."

There is a great deal of power in simply displaying your own relaxed attitude rather than telling someone that they ought to relax and be like you. One mild warning: the more natural and at ease that you are in front of someone shy, the more he may feel that he really is alone. He might think, "Everyone is relaxed and having a good time but me; what's wrong with me?" For that reason it is important to combine several of the ideas explained in this section, such as sharing your own apprehensiveness, touching, and the other tips presented below.

Gestures

Certain gestures can give a shy person a feeling of acceptance and a subtle message that you value them without putting them in the spotlight. It is not difficult to do; it simply takes awareness and sensitivity to a person's frame of mind. These are gestures that send the right message:

- reassuring nods;
- open hand movements that give the person a feeling of being included, especially if there are other people present;

- eye contact that, while not singling the person out, makes him feel as involved as everyone else in the immediate group; and
- a physical stance that includes the shy person without putting him center stage.

Validating the Other Person

Offer specific comments of validation. If your statements are phony, they are, of course, not going to be helpful. People who suffer from high levels of anxiety are especially perceptive and very sensitive to the genuineness of others. The key is simply to help the person remember the positive qualities that they have.

For example, if you see a man standing in the corner of the room at a party, it might be that he has forgotten every good thing about himself and every positive thing he has ever achieved in life. By offering a validating statement as you approach him, you can help him reintegrate some of the positive qualities which form the basis for self-esteem. You might say: "Mary tells me that you are quite a good tennis player. I wish I knew how you find the time to play with all of the other things you accomplish."

This is not a cheap or fake technique to make someone feel better; it is a genuine and helpful reminder that he is a valuable person even if he is experiencing some social discomfort. If you simply go up to someone and say something flattering without understanding the intention behind it, it would be little more than manipulation.

If your motives are good, in the sense that you genuinely want to help put others at ease, (perhaps because you also have suffered as they do), then the specific methods discussed here can have a very positive effect.

RESISTANCE TO REACHING OUT

There may be occasions when, in spite of your desire to help others, you hesitate to approach a person who seems shy.

You may think that the person's manner is standoffish,

and so you may have a natural impulse to stay away. I remember one occasion when, at a party, a friend came over to me saying, "Did you meet the iceberg, Cynthia, yet? She really seems snobbish; like she's too good to speak to anyone."

Sometimes, this kind of unresponsive person may be just trying to cover up her social anxiety. Rather than seeing this quality as a personality characteristic, it is important to see it as a defense against social encounters—just as you may have done in your own struggle with social anxiety. Of course, it is not your job to play therapist, but it is usually safe to assume that self-confident people do not present themselves in a cold and distant manner. If you react only to the surface behavior, you may not only feel resentful but also be unwilling to make an effort to help put that person at ease.

Look beyond the person's behavior and maintain your attempts at connecting with them; at least for a while. In the case of Cynthia, what my friend did not know was that Cynthia's girlfriend practically had to drag her to the party because she was so afraid to go. When I finally got up the courage to speak to her, it was a pleasant surprise that she was not snobbish at all, but in fact quite friendly behind her facade.

You may also resist making an effort to put someone at ease because you're afraid they may not respond to you the way you want them to, or that they will resent your approach or efforts no matter how genuine. Although this reaction can sometimes occur—some shy people may be too afraid to respond positively to you no matter how sincere and skillful you are—you must decide for yourself that it is a chance you are willing to take. Simply say to yourself, "This is something that I want to do; I value my efforts to help someone feel more at ease and the most I can do is try. If the other person doesn't respond in a positive way, it's not personal and I have at least tried." As the French writer Denis Diderot said, "Isn't it better to have a man be ungrateful than to miss a chance to do good?"

We all lose when some members of our society are unable to effectively share what they have and who they are with us because they fear rejection. We can help each other (as well as ourselves) by making a sincere effort to be open with each other and sensitive to those who may need more encouragement to accept themselves and to feel at ease.

This invitation may go against an ingrained competitive instinct that tells us to put the other person on the spot while we never let them see us sweat. That's nothing but a power game and I am suggesting that it is time that this attitude is challenged. We have more to offer each other through encouragement, sensitivity, and understanding than through intimidation; and our society has greater potential culturally and economically by helping each member to contribute fully than by allowing its shyer, more awkward ones to live lives of isolation and often despair. How can any of us be always at ease if all of us are not always at ease?

APPENDIXES

Recommended Associations
The Anxiety Disorders Association of America makes available to the public a national directory listing individuals and organizations that help people with anxiety disorders. Call or write to the Anxiety Disorders Association of America, 6000 Executive Blvd., #200, Rockville, MD 20852-4004, 301/231-9350.

Dr. McCullough has certified mental health consultants throughout the United States who offer telephone instruction for individuals suffering with anxiety, including social anxiety and agoraphobia. For information, please write to Dr. Christopher J. McCullough, 1592 Union Street, Box 191, San Francisco, CA 94123.

Recommended Books

Beck, Aron J., and Gary Emery. *Anxiety Disorders and Phobias.* New York: Basic Books, Inc., 1985.

Borysenko, Joan. *Minding the Body, Mending the Mind.* Reading, MA: Addison-Wesley, Inc., 1987.

Bowlby, John. *Separation.* New York: Basic Books, 1973.

Bradshaw, John. *Healing the Shame That Binds You.* Deerfield Beach, FL: Health Communication, Inc., 1988.

Branden, Nathaniel. *The Disowned Self.* New York: Bantam Books, 1973.

———. *Honoring the Self.* Los Angeles: Jeremy P. Tarcher, Inc., 1983.

———. *How To Raise Your Self-Esteem.* Toronto: Bantam Books, 1987.

Bright, Deborah. *The Official Criticism Manual.* New York: DB Publisher, 1991.

Burns, David. *Feeling Good.* New York: Signet, 1981.

Butler, Pamela. *Talking To Yourself.* San Francisco: Harper and Row, 1981.

Cheek, Jonathan. *Conquering Shyness.* New York: Putnam, 1989.

Elgin, Suzette H. *The Gentle Art of Verbal Self-Defense.* New York: Prentice-Hall, Inc., 1980.

Elsea, Janet. *First Impression, Best Impression.* New York: Simon and Schuster, Inc., 1984.

Fiore, Neil. *The Now Habit.* Los Angeles: Jeremy P. Tarcher, Inc., 1989.

Goldstein, Allan. *Overcoming Agoraphobia.* New York: Penguin Books, 1987.

Hamlin, Sonya. *How To Talk So People Listen.* New York: Harper and Row, 1988.

Handley, Robert and Pauline Neff. *Anxiety and Panic Attacks.* New York: Rawson Associates, 1985.

Henley, Arthur. *Phobias: The Crippling Fears.* New York: Avon Books, 1987.

Hochheiser, Robert. *How To Work For a Jerk.* New York: Vintage Books, 1987.

Hoff, Ron. *I Can See You Naked.* Kansas City: Andrews and McMeel, 1988.

Jeffers, Susan. *Feel the Fear and Do It Anyway.* New York: Fawcett Columbine, 1987.

McAdams, Dan. *Intimacy.* New York: Doubleday, 1989.

McKay, Matthew and Patrick Fanning. *Self-Esteem.* Oakland, CA: New Harbinger, 1986.

May, Rollo. *The Discovery of Being.* New York: W. W. Norton and Company, 1983.

———. *Man's Search For Himself.* New York: W. E. Norton and Company, 1953.

Miller, Sherod, et al. *Straight Talk.* New York: Signet, 1981.

Neuman, Fredric. *Fighting Fear.* New York: Macmillan, 1985.

Powell, Barbara. *Overcoming Shyness.* New York: McGraw-Hill, 1981.

Rainer, Tristine. *The New Diary.* Los Angeles: Jeremy P. Tarcher, Inc. 1979.

RoAne, Susan. *How To Work A Room.* New York: Shapolsky, Inc., 1988.

Rubin, Theodore I. *Compassion and Self-Hate.* New York: Macmillan, 1975.

Sarnoff, Dorothy. *Never Be Nervous Again.* New York: Crown Publishers, Inc., 1987.

Seagrave, Ann and Faison Covington. *Free From Fear.* New York: Pocket Books, 1987.

Smith, Manuel. *When I Say No I Feel Guilty.* New York: Bantam, 1975.

Waggoner, Glen, and Kathleen Maloney. *Esquire Etiquette.* New York: Macmillan, 1987.

Wells, Joel. *Who Do You Think You Are?* Chicago: Thomas More Press, 1989.

Wilson, Reid. *Don't Panic.* New York: Perennial Library, 1986.

Wurman, Richard Saul. *Information Anxiety.* New York: Doubleday, 1989.

Zimbardo, Philip. *Shyness.* Reading, MA: Addison-Wesley, Inc., 1977.